the GRAMMAR of UNTOLD STORIES

the GRAMMAR of UNTOLD STORIES

essays by

Lois Ruskai Melina

Shanti Arts Publishing
Brunswick, Maine

The Grammar of Untold Stories

Published by Shanti Arts Publishing

Cover and interior design by Shanti Arts Designs

Shanti Arts LLC
Brunswick, Maine
www.shantiarts.com

Printed in the United States of America

Cover image: Roger Peet, *Elementary.*
Used with permission of the artist.

ISBN: 978-1-951651-41-1 (softcover)
ISBN: 978-1-951651-42-8 (digital)

Library of Congress Control Number: 2020944078

for Oliver and Eleanor

also by Lois Ruskai Melina

Raising Adopted Children

Making Sense of Adoption

The Open Adoption Experience
(with Sharon Kaplan Roszia)

By a Fraction of a Second

The Embodiment of Leadership (Ed.)

Contents

Acknowledgments & Notes

Lidia Yuknavitch, I am so grateful for whatever it is you conjure in your Corporeal Writing workshops that allowed me to find my voice and take risks and have the confidence to send these essays into the world.

Laura Stride, Anne Gudger, Anne Falkowski, Mary Mandeville, Christie O. Tate, Tanya Friedman, Amanda Niehaus, Janeen Armstrong, Jane Gregorie, Sue Moshovsky, Barry Netzley, Anatoly Molotkov, Michael Keefe, Margaret Pinard, Zinn Adeline, Joe Oestreich, Louella Bryant, and, of course, Lidia: I deeply appreciate the thought you gave to the essays you read. Your feedback helped strengthen them, your support sustained me.

Carl, you not only read and commented on the messy first drafts and all the revisions, you've believed in me as a writer for a long time.

•

I am grateful to the editors of the following journals for publishing these essays, in some cases with slight variations from the way they appear in this collection:

2016 Best of the Net Anthology (Sundress Publications): "Down in the River to Pray"

Blood Orange Review: "Metamorphosis," Spring 2017

The Carolina Quarterly: "Fires of Dismemberment," Winter 2017

Chattahoochee Review: "Boulders," Fall 2017/Winter 2018

Colorado Review: "The Grammar of Untold Stories," Fall 2017/ Winter 2018

Crab Orchard Review: "The Scent of Water," June 2019

Eastern Iowa Review: "Wings," March 1, 2019

Entropy: "Beyond Mt. St. Helens," April 9, 2018; "Still Life with Birds," March 20, 2018

Fourth and Sycamore: "Species, Genus, Family, Order," July 8, 2016

Literary Mama: "The Four Seasons of Longing," October 2016

Lunch Ticket: "Down in the River to Pray," Summer/Fall 2016

Sport Literate: "The Synchronicity of Healing," 2019

Two Hawks Quarterly: "On Finding Myself in the Old Neighborhood," November 18, 2019

•

Though some of the pieces in this collection were first published as poems and one as a short story, they were all conceived and written as essays from memory held in my body. I believe them to be true representations of my experience. In some cases, names and identifying details have been changed to protect the privacy of the individuals introduced and discussed in these essays.

FAMILY

Metamorphosis

To find a star garnet:
First, drive to the Idaho Panhandle National Forests. Alternatively, go to India.

You will need to bring a shovel, a bucket, heavy plastic bags, and an eighteen-inch square made of two-by-fours with a quarter-inch screen stretched over one open side.

Take a child too. A ten-year-old is best. A seven-year-old may get bored and start throwing rocks.

Think twice about taking your mother, even if she is visiting from the city where she has lived most of her life, where she takes your children to the zoo when they come to visit even though they have seen bear and moose from the trails they've hiked and coyote and deer and quail from their bedroom windows. You will be tempted to want to show her who you are, who you've become since leaving the city—someone who knows her way around screes and cedar, who can smell the musk of a rutting elk in the autumn woods, identify a huckleberry bush bare of fruit, track a wounded deer in the snow.

Keeping your eyes on the road as you drive down Idaho Highway 3, explain to your mother and your children that the ground beneath you is part of a vast glacial flood plain.

Say this: "At the end of the last Ice Age, creeping glacial ice blocked the Clark Fork River in what is now northern Idaho and northwestern Montana, forming a lake 2,000 feet deep and 200 miles wide. When the ice dam failed, water flowed out faster than cars on a freeway, tossing boulders, carving out gullies and coulees, piling up rocks, creating valleys and waterfalls and basins." When no one responds, keep talking. Fill the emptiness with what you know, with words. Explain that the rolling hills of the Camas Prairie are ripples from the force of that water washing through. The scablands of eastern Washington were carved by it, and the Palouse River was pushed away from its confluence with the Columbia River and forced to drop over a shelf on its new journey to the Snake. Grapes in the Willamette River Valley of Oregon flourish today in the fertile silt deposited in that flood.

Take a breath before going on: "The ice moved again, dammed the river again, flooded the land again and again, creating the landscape from the west slope of the Rocky Mountains to the Pacific Ocean. The basin of this former lake is where you can find fossils of fish and where minerals like garnets that were heavy enough and strong enough and deep enough to withstand that kind of battering are just beneath the surface, waiting to be found if you dig a little bit."

Turn onto the Forest Service road that leads to the stretch of Emerald Creek where you are allowed to search for gemstones. Follow the creek as it meanders through the meadow at the edge of the trees. Point out how ordinary it seems, how it gives no clue of the treasures it holds close. You will pass a mill where they crush garnets into abrasives for fine sandpaper. The pink sand will dust your tires and stick to the lower parts of your car, sparkling in the sun. Be careful when you wash it off—it can scratch the finish.

Buy your one-day permit.

As you walk single file from the car to the creek, smelling the freshness of yellow pine in the woods, explain to your mother and children that metamorphic rocks are formed by change. Say this: "Heat and pressure deep in the underworld of the Earth alter the texture and composition of rocks. The pressure breaks bonds and causes minerals to recrystallize into structures that are stable in this hot, stressful environment. Garnets are a family of minerals formed this way." Recite the geological names of all the minerals in the garnet group: almandite, grossular, pyrope, spessartite, andradite, and uvarovite. Tell them garnets can be red, green, yellow, brown, purple, even—rarely—blue, but in Idaho, the stones are mostly deep red like the seeds of pomegranates. Reveal the purpose of this excavation: "What is unique to the garnets of northern Idaho and India is that some contain tiny rods of rutile— another mineral—that lie along the crystal planes of the stone. When the polished dome of a garnet is turned under the sun, these rods reflect light, making a four-ray 'star' that looks like an 'X' or six-ray that looks like an asterisk." Raise both your arms, even though you are carrying a shovel and a screen, to punctuate your declaration: "This is what we're looking for."

With the shovel, dig up the loose gravel from the creek bed and put it in the bucket. When the bucket is full, spill a little of it onto the screen. Dip the screen in the creek and wash the smaller stones out. Sort through the larger rocks for one that is the color of the skin of ripe plums. It will be rough, not showing its full potential. Take that rock and toss it in the palm of your hand. Feel the weight of it. Then you'll know. Examine it for fractures. If there are too many, put it back in the river. When you find a stone that is big enough and without serious fault, place it in a plastic bag to take home.

Your mother will not have the right shoes for walking off trail. She will not know how to pee in the woods, so she will refuse to drink water. She will sit on a log a ways from the creek, too far to be included, too far to see you or your children stand in the creek, the frigid meltwater swirling around your ankles until your feet are numb. She will smile, the way a houseguest does, and speak only to say, "No, I'm fine here," or "Aren't you worried he's going to hit someone with those rocks," or "Oh, my," when your daughter shows her the mound of rocks she has pocketed as worthy.

After you fill all the bags, or your feet are cold, or even your ten-year-old has started throwing rocks, go back to the car. Drive out of the woods, past the mill, into the meadow, and find a spot where you can sit on the bank of the creek and eat lunch. Park the car where your mother can sit in the passenger seat and still see you while she eats.

As you pass out sandwiches and fish out cans of soda floating in the melting ice of your cooler, explain that the word "garnet" is derived from Latin words for grain and pomegranate. Say this: "As rocks metamorphose, garnets begin as tiny grains, then grow over time as metamorphosis continues, sometimes becoming included in rock. The polished gems were used in Egyptian jewelry. Noah is said to have used a garnet lantern to steer the Ark. Early explorers carried them as talismans."

Look in the creek while you are eating in case there is a garnet reflecting aubergine in the clear water.

On the way home, after the children have fallen asleep, tell your mother that a psychic told you once to wear a large garnet ring as protection and that you had a fifteen-carat garnet with a four-pointed star—one you found in Emerald Creek—polished and fashioned into a sterling silver setting. Say this: "It looks like something the pope might have on his finger."

Don't tell her that you wear it when you are afraid, when you aren't sure you can be the rock that she and your children expect you to be.

For Mother's Day, have one of the stones you found polished into a cabochon. Choose one about four carats in weight. Have it made into a lapel pin suitable for a Pendleton wool blazer. Give it to your mother to remember the day she went to Emerald Creek to pan for garnets.

Down in the River to Pray

This is what I knew:

My nephew Benji graduated from drama school. When he crossed the stage to accept his diploma, he wore a sultry Lauren Bacall wig and a cream-colored satin evening gown with padded shoulders. His make-up was perfect, his lips the color of blood and desire. My mother told me he looked stunning. And that after the ceremony he argued with his father and my sister, his stepmother but the mother who raised him.

Then he left for New York.

It was 1988.

Fourteen years later, my mother told me Benji had disappeared. He came home one day from his job at a restaurant and trashed the apartment he shared with a roommate. Then he left. No one knew how to find him or if he was even alive.

Her voice dropped to a whisper as she added, "He has HIV."

I put a story together that, at the time, didn't need to be correct; it just needed to be a story that made sense. I thought "estranged." I thought "We don't know where Benji is" meant Benji moved and changed his phone number because he didn't want to talk to his family any more. Many of us have been on one side or the other of that wall, but we know it's a wall that exists because we agree to it. We know we can find or be found if necessary. And six years after Benji disappeared, it was necessary that I find him.

I needed to find Benji because my mother died and left Benji and her other grandchildren a little money. Because she didn't know what happened to Benji, she stipulated that the money would go to "living grandchildren." If Benji wasn't alive, his share went to the eight other grandchildren, not to his father, his next-of-kin.

As my mother's executor, I had to find Benji if he was still alive.

I thought about the last time I'd seen Benji. It was the mid-1990s. I was in New York for business. We met at a restaurant near the Met. He didn't mind coming uptown, he told me when he picked the restaurant. His face was freshly washed, and he wore a shirt with an open collar. It must have been fall because I remember us eating at a table on the sidewalk and Benji wearing a brown tweed sport coat.

Benji held his fork in his left hand while he cut the pork cutlet, then switched his fork to his right hand to take a bite, the way he'd learned growing up in the Midwest; he hadn't adopted any big city cutlery affectations.

"I'm still waiting tables," he said, when I asked what he was doing.

"But I'm rehearsing a play," he added, slurring his words like a Chicagoan does.

I smiled. "That's great. How often do you perform?"

He shrugged and stabbed another piece of pork, holding it on his fork, suspended in front of his mouth while he answered. "It's just some people I know—in this warehouse space, but I think it could lead to some auditions."

I noticed his sport coat didn't fit well, and I thought he probably bought it at a thrift store just for our lunch. I didn't know how Benji usually dressed, whether the satin gown at his graduation was to shock his parents, upstage his drama school classmates, or to come out. Maybe he didn't own a sport coat because he didn't lunch uptown that often. Maybe he didn't wear men's clothes. At the time, I assumed he thought I would feel more comfortable if he didn't look showy, and I had been oddly touched. My cheeks reddened at the memory of Benji considering my comfort when he got dressed that day. The idea that Benji might have covered his flamboyance for me was touching in the mid-1990s, embarrassing in 2008.

I hadn't been a very involved aunt. I was eighteen and Benji was five when my sister married Benji's father, a widower with five children. It's true that I was focused on college, on love, later on my own marriage, but I also avoided my sister, who could be dramatic, telling stories that were inconsistent with previous stories—and sometimes with reality. I could understand if Benji went dark just to avoid her.

I thought it would be easy to find Benji. We leave so many tracks: credit cards, tax returns, rental history, work records. A few phone calls and Google searches, and we can find a childhood sweetheart, a college roommate, a lost child.

But I was wrong; it wasn't easy.

We don't know where Benji is was not just parent code for *Benji doesn't want us to know where he is.* It wasn't just Benji code for *My father, a crew-cut cop, is uncomfortable around me because I wear make-up, and my mother lives in her own reality. So I am not going to make the trek home for Thanksgiving when I can make some good tips if I stay in New York and wait tables.*

All of that may have been true, except that Benji really had disappeared.

•

By the time Benji arrived in New York in 1988, more than 22,000 people in the city had been diagnosed with AIDS. The records from that time don't distinguish between HIV positive and AIDS. They don't distinguish male or female, black or white. They don't break the numbers down by neighborhood, age, or method of transmission. They document diagnosis and death. At the end of that year, just over a third of those ever diagnosed were still alive.

•

I'd been an investigative journalist and an academic researcher. I had skills—information finding skills, people-finding skills. I knew how to dig, uncover what was buried. This is what I found:

Social Security did not list Benji as deceased. The last address they had for him was the apartment he'd left a mess.

He was not listed among New York City inmates.

No criminal or civil charges had been filed against him, not for panhandling or prostitution or assault or anything.

He was not listed as a sex offender in the state of New York.

He'd last been treated at Bellevue Hospital as an outpatient in early 2002; as an inpatient the previous year.

His Medicaid card was expired.

There had been no death report for someone with his name in a public place nor of someone with his name having been taken from a public place to a hospital in any of the boroughs that make up Manhattan.

They could check by description: *In 2002, Benji was thirty-six years old. He was five foot eight, slim, but not an athletic build. His skin was white. His hair was brown, his eyes were hazel. His eyelashes were long. He had long fingers. His features were delicate. He looked like he wouldn't be able to grow a beard, but he could get a surprising five o'clock shadow. He had a big smile with large teeth that had never known orthodontics.*

They said there were no reports of anyone with that description.

•

I didn't want to talk to my sister or her husband about Benji. I didn't want to go into their pain. I didn't know what the story was that they had decided they could live with or how much of it was true. I wanted to find Benji without talking to either of them, but my sister called me. She knew what the will said.

"We didn't know Benji was missing until two months after

24

he left his apartment," my sister said, adding that they found out when his boss called to say he had Benji's last paycheck and wanted to know where he should send it. My sister immediately called Benji's roommate who told her about the damage and gave her the number of a friend who'd helped Benji move his things to a self-storage locker. My sister's voice took on a tone I recognized from the time when she was a teenager about to tell a secret to me, seven years younger. It's the tone of voice a soap opera character uses just before they cut to commercial. "She said he might be living at the storage locker, but no one had seen him for weeks. They were all very worried."

I imagined what I would have felt if I were the parent remembering the argument the last time I'd spoken to my son, the angry parting, emptiness, loss, longing, an ache that I would have woken up to each morning—sometimes not right away, sometimes after a few minutes of feeling like the world was normal, the conversations over whether to call him or wait for him to call.

I thought about Benji living in a five-by-five-foot windowless storage unit. I tried to imagine a scenario in which he could have lived for six years with untreated HIV, without the kind of job that reported earnings, without ever being picked up on the streets because he had the kind of income that doesn't come with Social Security contributions.

My sister told me she and her husband looked for him as soon as they heard he was missing. They drove from Chicago to New York. His father staked out the self-storage locker. I imagined him sitting in a rented car, maybe a Ford Taurus, by himself, sipping coffee and eating take-out burgers, replaying old conversations, rehearsing the one he might have.

After a week, Benji's father talked to the police, one cop to another. No, he didn't want to file a missing person report.

Then they went home to Chicago.

"I called the storage place six months later," my sister said. "They told me Benji's things had been auctioned. No one had paid the fees. They never even let us know to come and get them."

Before we hung up, my sister told me the story she believed, the story that I knew didn't have to be true as long as it made sense: "I think he threw himself off a bridge."

•

I called Benji's younger sister, the sibling he was closest to, the way the oldest sometimes is with the youngest. The one he would trust to lie to their parents when they asked her if she'd heard from him.

"I really don't know where he is," she told me. "The last time I saw him was a little more than a year before he disappeared. I went to New York to visit him. He'd changed. I mean, he was a real jerk. As I got into a cab to go to the airport, I told him so. I said, 'I'm not going to come back if you're going to be an asshole.'"

"Fuck you."

"I talked to him after that, though," she said. "Once, right after 9/11." He was OK. She told him she loved him. That was the last time she talked to him. She was quiet, and I thought maybe I could hear her weeping, so I talked.

"Do you remember the time I visited? It was during the Olympics. Oh gosh, you must have been eight, and we all went to the pool, and you and Benji pretended to be synchronized swimmers." I described the two of them diving into the water then bursting out with exaggerated smiles and arms extended, then submerging again to do handstands on the bottom of the pool, their legs extending above the surface and scissor-kicking, nowhere near synchronized.

"I'll find him," I told her.

I flew to New York.

His apartment—his last known address—was on the East Side, near the East Village, in a dirty yellow brick building above a space that's been a sandwich shop, a Thai restaurant, and a vegan cafe. He could walk from there to Bellevue.

Benji's roommate in that apartment had moved, but I found her. It wasn't that hard. She asked me to meet her at a park near the East River. We sat on a bench where we could see the Brooklyn Bridge. It was October, but warm enough to sit outside without a coat, even with the breeze off the water. The sun was sharp, and we both wore sunglasses. I noticed we also both wore black. I hadn't paid attention to that when I dressed, but it was obvious, the two of us sitting side-by-side on the bench as though in a pew.

She lit a cigarette and took a drag. "We met at the restaurant where we worked. We usually worked different shifts so it made it easy to share a flat. We weren't what you'd call 'friends.' Benji had his own friends—artists and other actors." She flicked her ash. "Most of them were waiting tables too."

He'd been hospitalized for AIDS-related pneumonia the year before he disappeared, she said, but he'd gotten better and been re-classified as HIV positive. She dropped the butt of her cigarette and ground it cold. "He was getting treatment, but he was starting to get paranoid."

I turned toward her. "What do you mean?" She took a deep breath. "Benji was a good roommate. He didn't cook much, but like, he always cleaned up the kitchen—even if I was the one who left it a mess. We often slept at different times, and he was quiet. Considerate of that, you know?" She reached in her purse for another cigarette, but didn't light it.

I nodded. "He was always good with his younger brothers and sister," I said, "willing to play with them and be silly."

She fumbled with the cigarette. "Then he started accusing his friends of all kinds of shit—like saying he didn't get parts he'd auditioned for because other actors had trash-talked him. I came home one day and found everything in the kitchen broken. He'd slashed his mattress with this huge carving knife. He'd pulled everything off the walls." She lit the cigarette.

I imagined Benji tearing down a poster of a Mapplethorpe photograph, the kind you can find rolled up for quick sale from any of a dozen street vendors, tearing it into strips. I thought about him throwing a jar of mustard at the wall. It shatters. He is surprised at how the thick liquid dulls the sound of glass on wall. He expected something like the clear tinkling of a breaking window when a baseball hits it. He was no good at baseball. I think about him grabbing a bottle of PBR from the shelf of the refrigerator, knocking the neck on the counter. The bottle breaking jagged, below the cap, him lifting it to his lips and drinking, the points of brown glass piercing his lips, blood staining his mouth, the taste of beer and blood, the rustiness running down his chin. He throws the empty bottle at a row of spice jars above the stove. The cheaply made rack, held only by a single nail, falls to the stove, spices mixing with alcohol in the shallow pans under the coils of the electric stove, the smells of cinnamon and cloves and nutmeg mingled with hops reminding him of Thanksgiving at his parents'—pumpkin pie and bad beer.

She let the ash gather on the cigarette, not smoking. "And he wrote something on the wall above his bed in this really red lipstick." She wrote in the air, as though using the ash of the cigarette to make words: "*If you want to know why, call my parents. And he wrote their phone number.*"

I didn't ask her why she didn't call. "Do you know how I can reach any of his friends?" She gave me the number for James. She said he was a painter.

I stood up. "Thank you for coming," I said. We hugged. She started to walk off, then stopped and turned. "You'll let me know if you hear anything."

"Of course."

•

In 2002, people were living with HIV. It had been more than ten years since Freddie Mercury died of AIDS, more than ten years since Magic Johnson announced he was HIV positive. In New York City alone, more than 62,000 men were living with a diagnosis of HIV/AIDS. Fewer than 2,000 of them died that year.

Record-keeping became more sophisticated, statistics more detailed. In 2002, Benji was one of thirty-three men in his neighborhood who were HIV positive, without AIDS. Probably one of a dozen white men.

•

Before calling James, I looked him up on the internet. He'd had one or two shows in small but good galleries. I scrolled through the images. They were grotesque. Distorted. Open wounds. Blood on chin.

I met him on a bench in the plaza by St. Mark's Church. Pigeons collected at our feet, looking for handouts. Leaves swirled with the light breeze. James wore expensive jeans. Cashmere scarf. His nails were recently manicured. Lots of product in his bleached blonde hair.

I wanted to ask so many things—things I didn't need to know to find Benji, but wanted to know, to feel that I knew him, and somehow that seemed wrong, like I'd had my chance to know Benji and I would just look curious, like someone gawking at the scene of an accident.

I pulled a red pashmina from my bag and wrapped it around me. "I didn't see Benji very often, but I remember that he asked me to dance at my wedding," I said. "He was nine and very awkward, but he took it very seriously." James smiled. "He was a terrible dancer," he said. We laughed.

I asked him about his art and if he'd ever painted Benji. If he said yes, I knew I would offer to buy the painting. He knew it, too. He shook his head. "No," he said too quickly. "I wanted to. He had this vulnerability, this softness." He closed his eyes as though imagining Benji before he turned violent. "He never let me."

He crossed his legs. "The irony," James said, "was that Benji had just qualified for Medicaid. He was excited to be able to get treatment." He paused, and I waited out the silence. "But he was becoming very erratic—fine one day and the next day just plain mean." He fought with all his friends. Burned a lot of bridges. "We weren't surprised when he lost it that day at the apartment," James said. "We all knew it was the disease, or maybe the drugs. I mean, it wasn't the real Benji, but most people couldn't take it after a while.

"Benji called me from the apartment that day and said he had to get out of his place," James said. He showed up with AJ, who worked with Benji at the restaurant and could get the catering van. They loaded Benji's things, whatever they could carry that he hadn't broken, and drove to a warehouse with storage units. On the way, Benji gave James his watch. He gave AJ something too. James didn't remember what. He uncrossed his legs and crossed them again. "I offered him a place to crash. AJ did too. But Benji said to leave him at the warehouse."

James looked at the birds gathered at his feet. I heard him swallow and take a breath. "I called the police and asked what we should do if we saw Benji on the street and he was acting crazy." He looked up, towards the sky above the church. "They said not to approach him."

We sat quietly for a while, then James stood up to leave. "You should talk to AJ," he said as he gave me a drive-by hug. "He was the last person to see Benji."

•

New cases of AIDS peaked in New York City in 1993 and 1994. Benji was twenty-eight years old then.

•

I called my husband and told him I would be staying in New York a little longer.

"Are you getting somewhere?" he asked.

"Not really. The trail's pretty cold."

I told him what the police at the precinct told me: Hundreds of men in their mid-thirties died every year in New York City and remained unidentified. If a missing person report had been filed, they might have connected one of them, but probably not.

"Benji isn't even a cold case," I said.

"Why didn't his dad file a missing person report?" my husband asked.

"I don't know. It wouldn't help me find Benji now," I answered.

"You know, Lo . . ." My husband's voice was tender. "If Benji had AIDS-related dementia, and he wasn't being treated, odds are he's dead." My husband is a physician, and he took care of the first case of AIDS in the small town we lived in during the 1980s. No one else would.

"I know," I said. "I'm starting to think my sister's right—that Benji was depressed or psychotic and jumped off a bridge. There's just no trace of him."

Benji alive but missing made closing my mother's estate more difficult, but my job as executor, my feelings as Benji's aunt, and my attraction to tracking down answers to difficult questions had become jumbled. I didn't want Benji to be dead. I also didn't want to learn that some of my sister's stories were true; it was easier to believe she consistently made things up.

"Maybe you should come home," he suggested, still tender.

"I kind of feel like maybe I'm doing some good just by meeting with his friends. They seem to get something out of talking about him. So do I. He just disappeared. No one had any closure."

"Why didn't his parents have him declared dead?" my husband asked.

"Probably they just wanted to hang onto a little hope," I said.

"Well, if you're hanging onto hope, wouldn't you file a missing person report?"

I didn't answer.

Hope, someone told me once, is believing in the best possible outcome without any evidence to support it. Some people don't find comfort in hope; they find peace by ending the ambiguity and uncertainty. They create a story with an ending. They would hold a memorial service where family and friends could talk about the person the way they wanted to remember him— his smile, his generosity, his innocence. They would console one another. Embrace. They would have a meal together. They would laugh at the funny stories about him and wonder if it was okay to laugh. The way I was doing with Benji's friends.

•

The restaurant Benji worked at had closed. AJ had a job at a different restaurant, an Italian place in the Village. He said I could meet him

31

there before the place opened for dinner. He unlocked the door for me and led me to a square table with a red-checked tablecloth. He brought me a plate of lasagna and a green salad with vinegar and oil dressing. "You want some wine?" he asked. I did. He brought me something red and put a small arrangement of chrysanthemums on the center of the table. They smelled like Homecoming.

I picked up my fork and took a bite of the pasta. The cheese stretched from my fork to the plate. I spun my fork to break it off. I didn't feel hungry, but I appreciated AJ's thoughtfulness and tried to eat. The cheese was hot. The sauce rich with garlic and basil. A little sweet—a sauce with a little sugar. I stabbed some lettuce.

"No one saw Benji for a week after he moved to the warehouse," AJ said. "One day he walked into the restaurant, through the door that led from the alley to the kitchen. He was still wearing the green cotton T-shirt he had on when we dropped him at the storage locker." I imagined it pitted and stained, the sourness of his unwashed skin mingled with the cloying smell of weed clinging to his clothes. His eyes bloodshot. A week's worth of stubble. His hair unwashed and stringy. I could picture him standing in the kitchen, all stainless steel and clean white tile.

AJ picked up a fork and turned it around in his hands. "I thought the boss would tell Benji to get out, to go home and take a shower, get some sleep. But he put down the knife he was sharpening and reached under his white apron into his pocket and pulled out a silver clip with some bills. He took the bills out, licked his fingers, then culled a series of twenties from the pack." I imagined the bills as freshly starched and ironed as the chef's apron. AJ continued: "He held out the money to Benji and told him to take as much time off as he needed."

Benji grabbed the bills. He threw them in the air as though they were ticker tape. He looked up at them and laughed as they drifted to the freshly washed floor. For a moment, he looked like a child. Then he looked at the boss and narrowed his eyes. "I don't want your fucking money," he said, and walked out. "I went after him," AJ said, "but he told me not to come near him." No one saw him after that.

I asked AJ if Benji had anyone special.

He dropped his head. "Not really. Everyone loved Benji." The way he said it, I knew AJ loved him more.

I apologized for not being able to eat. I told AJ I didn't have much of an appetite. He nodded. I took a sip of wine, but I was still looking at AJ when I put the glass down and set it partially on the salad plate. The glass wobbled before I caught it, but some of the wine splashed onto the newly laundered tablecloth.

I stood up. "I'm so sorry." He stood up. I touched his shoulder. He wrapped his arms around me. I waited for him to pull away. His eyes were wet. Like mine.

•

Between 1990 and 2004, there were 2,272 suicides by residents of Manhattan. Seventy percent were males. Almost sixty percent were white. Twenty-two percent were in Benji's age range.

Ninety percent chose falling, hanging, overdosing, shooting, or getting run over by a train.

Only eight percent were found in an outdoor location other than their residence.

Nonresidents—those who travel to New York to commit suicide—are far more likely than residents to jump off a bridge into water.

The police don't keep records of people who jump off bridges. They would tell an unreliable story. Not all the bodies surface.

Impact, not drowning, is thought to kill most. The body hits the water at eighty miles per hour, shattering bones and brain and internal organs. Like getting hit by a train.

•

I called the attorney handling my mother's estate and told him to send a registered letter to Benji's father: "We all hope and pray that one day we will find Benji, but we are distributing the estate with the assumption that Benji is deceased."

After, I walked by myself to the middle of the Brooklyn Bridge. It wasn't the closest bridge to Benji's apartment or to the warehouse or the restaurant, but it was the most popular bridge for suicides, even though it wasn't the highest. Perhaps people choose it because with its granite and limestone arches like windows in a medieval church, it is the most graceful.

The wind was blowing, and the air off the East River was cooler than it had been. It smelled of fish and diesel. I pulled a long black chiffon scarf from around my neck and draped it over my head, crossing it under my chin and tying it behind my neck. With my dark glasses, I might have looked like a 1960s movie star.

I thought I could feel the bridge sway a bit as I walked in the pedestrian aisle, a level above the cars, and I wondered if it was the wind or the traffic or my imagination. Or maybe it was me that was unsteady.

Near one of the stone arches, I stopped and opened my purse to pull out a tube of the most scarlet lipstick I found earlier in the day at Macy's. I leaned against the rock as I applied the lipstick, tracing lips from memory. Then I looked out over the river at the ferries and tugboats. Below, I knew, the water eddied around the column that reached deep below the surface. I gripped the railing. The metal felt smooth and hard and cold.

I walked to the middle of the expanse, to the lowest point in the parabolic curve formed by the cables that connect the bridge to its supports.

I wondered if the wind blew that day, and if it was cold.

I wondered if it was dark.

I wondered if Benji looked at the skyline of a city he thought would fulfill his dreams.

If he closed his eyes.

I wondered how long he stood there before climbing over the railing onto the steel beams that extend out over the water. Before he walked to the edge.

I wondered if a crowd gathered.

If anyone said a prayer.

The Four Seasons of Longing

If I'd had a baby in the fall, she would have hair the color of autumn leaves—red and gold. And I mean the red and gold of October in Ohio, not the wet yellow and muted orange of the Pacific Northwest where she would grow up, but the kind of hair that, when you see it, you pull off the road to take a picture. Moralovitz hair, which she would grow up disliking because relatives would tell her that her great-grandmother had hair like that and because it would be unruly and she wouldn't know it looked like fire framing her face when the sun was low in the sky, the way it is after the Equinox.

You have to choose a name carefully for a baby born in the fall; she will know loss early. Her name can't be frivolous or playful. It must be strong enough to bear the sudden darkness, the shock of leaves falling to the ground, their wonder now a chore, the speed at which fertility is overtaken by barrenness. But not a hopeless name because she would still be a child.

•

By the time I was a teenager, my abdominal cavity had been

overtaken by cells that had rebelled, bolting from my womb and growing into unruly scars. The lining of my uterus, luscious and pink where an embryo would cling and be nourished and become, fled instead, attaching where it didn't belong, turning me inside out.

•

If I'd had a baby in the winter, she would be born deep in darkness. A child who emerges when bear cubs and apples, more in sync with the seasons, wouldn't dare, is not timid. She would be bold and disregard convention, a child of extremes, of broken collarbones and a voice that wouldn't be carried off by the wind.

I would peek in her room while she sleeps and see her body shaped in opposing angles as though I were viewing an excavation of bones that had been lying beneath the earth for decades—maybe centuries—white and hard and fragile. I would feel again the sharpness of a shifting shoulder, an elbow, a heel—long nights when those bones poked at me.

Her skin would be thin and white, blue veins easily visible, and shiny, like the surface of a frozen pond, cheeks easily flushed by icy air or a gentle scolding.

I would want to protect her, keep her inside, not expose her to the sharp wind of a school bus stop or the slip of tires on black ice the first winter she could drive. When you come from darkness, your bones know it, welcome it. It can creep easily into the soul of a daring girl born in winter, the way a chill might settle into her after a fevered run down a feathered slope. She will need to learn how to turn her face to the light the way a peony planted in the shade of a ginkgo tree reaches for the sun.

•

By the time I was twenty-six, the adhesions reached into every part of my gut. I imagined them like the gauze cobwebs people buy to stretch over their shrubs at Halloween, one strand winding around an ovary then reaching for my colon, another filament choking a fallopian tube, another my vagina, my internal organs pulled out of whack.

•

A baby born in spring would be promise and pastels. She would want to be held, to have you brush her hair, even when she is too big and bony to sit on your lap. She is bare legs before the weather changes. She is the dank smell of damp ground. Another child might bring you a broken robin's egg, the softest blue on earth. She would carry the fledgling who tried to fly too soon, and you would watch her breathe air into its body, mouth to beak, quick bursts, faint whistle.

If I'd had a baby in the spring, she would laugh from her belly. People would seek her out when they need light and not know the price she pays to be the one they depend on to give them hope. Hope can be heavy, a burden for one so young. And you would not know how much because of her smile. Maybe there are dimples. Maybe not. It doesn't matter. Maybe you would see teeth, even if they were wired to one another to pull them straight when they tried to go astray.

If you see her shoulders start to fall, even a little, you must not tell her to stand up straight. You must go to her, pull her onto your lap, stroke her hair. Don't be afraid. She will let you. She will curl into you, the way her body remembers. She will even lay her head on your breast.

•

By the time I was thirty, everything hurt: my period, my bowel movements, sex, hope.

•

37

If I'd had a baby in the summer, she would come to life in the ocean. Waves would break over her. Sand would come home with her, between her toes, under her fingernails, in the labyrinth of her ears. It would stick to her scalp. The grit of her.

She is tide, inching higher and higher, taking up more and more beach, all foam and blue eyes, then receding into herself, leaving rocks exposed, wet, slippery. She is driftwood. Not a bleached white wood, but Pacific madrone, the color of salmon and the flesh of apples, heartwood as red as autumn leaves, grains and roughness smoothed by water.

A girl born in summer surprises you like a sneaker wave, and you have to hold on because she is stronger than she looks. And she will take you with her.

You will wonder if you ever really know her, if you ever see the full depth of her, and whether that is because she moves so quickly or because you are afraid of getting caught in her riptide, of being pulled under, because when that happens, you cannot fight, you have to just let go.

•

My uterus was a mine that would never deliver any gold. At thirty-two, I begged the gynecologist to take it out. He balked. "You will never be able to have children," he said, seated between the stirrups cradling my bare feet.

I answered, trying to keep my voice cool as a frozen pond, my blue eyes an ocean intent on the light above the table, blocked from the doctor's gaze by the sheet draped over the bones of my knees: "Not everyone wants children."

Across Time and Space

"Wake up, Peanut," my father said that May morning in 1961, our black-and-white Zenith TV tuned to live coverage of the 7:34 MDT launch of *Freedom 7*. He and I watched the preparations, Alan Shepard's walk to the rocket ship, the countdown, blast-off, the capsule separating from the launch rocket, the fifteen-minute flight. I sat cross-legged on the floor in my pajamas, back bent forward, holding my sleepy head in my hands. He sat in his swivel chair, smoking Kents, telling me to move back or I'd ruin my eyes.

He flicked an ash.

"This is history," he said, as Shepard hurtled home to Earth, his capsule splashing into the water of the Atlantic Ocean where it rocked him like a cradle.

•

On a Saturday the year before Alan Shepherd was launched into space, my father brought me to what he called "The Plant" on the outskirts of Littleton, Colorado, a rural area that rapidly grew into a town because of new manufacturing facilities like the one where my father worked, built to support the nascent space program and Cold War defense technology.

My father ushered me into a room. The air was cool, my father's hand in mine warm. We stood in the doorway, our long shadows pointing to something the size of a furnace, Army green and metal.

"It's a computer," my father said, with such pride I thought he'd invented it himself.

"This is the future."

I wonder if my eyes opened wide, if I asked him questions: What does it do? How does it work? I don't remember ever being interested in the way things work—mechanical advantages, resistance, friction, transistors, chips. I want to plug something in, turn a switch to "on," and have it function. Car. Microwave. Motion sensor light. How it works holds no attraction.

In the realm of science, only chemistry appealed to me. Not the lab work, with precise measurements and the need for protective goggles; I liked the way negatively charged elements with more electrons than protons reached out to elements with more protons than electrons, how they bonded to fill the emptiness in their outer shells, how the bonds made atoms more stable, whole.

Mostly, though, I was interested in stories. In families and cultures and societies. In what holds us together.

•

The earliest photographs of me with my father show his back bent over, frozen into a letter C. Attached to a metal back brace, a leather strap around his forehead is designed to pull his head up. He is an engineer. The brace is his invention. To look at the camera while standing, my father bends his knees and thrusts his hips down. Not seen: the vertebrae of his spine and neck fused together. Bony spurs extended from inflamed vertebrae and attached to adjacent ones. Bonded. Welded. Immovable.

At night, my father tucked me in, kneeling by my bed to tell me the next adventure of Ike and Mike and their little sister Evelyn Marie. I was entranced by stories of a family whose daily activities were so much like mine. It would be years before I realized they required no imagination—even the characters' names were barely disguised versions of those in our family. The best a mechanical engineer could do. It would be even later—after his death—before I understood that my father was in pain when he knelt by my bed, in pain when he walked, in pain when he lay in bed at the end of the day.

•

My father's blue Dodge had a series of angled mirrors across the top of the front windshield. He must have designed those too. Unable to turn his head, he used the mirrors when he drove alone. When I was in the passenger seat, it was my job to look and tell him when it was safe to pull into traffic. He trusted the mirrors. He trusted me. The things he created.

•

When I was born, my mother was anesthetized. My father waited in the hallway outside the delivery room, thin and curved, smoking the cigarettes that were already weakening the walls of his cerebral artery. I was fed bottled formula, which was considered a scientific advance over breast milk, the added iron and vitamin D thought to be worth sacrificing the emotional connection that develops from the skin-to-skin contact of a baby suckling at her mother's breast.

•

My husband, a family doctor, opened his office in 1979, a time when labor and delivery practices were changing. He spent his days talking with one expectant mother after another, each wanting to enhance bonding and attachment to her newborn

41

by remaining awake for the birth and having the father stand by to cut the cord. These mothers planned to hold their babies immediately after birth and nurse them.

This was not my future.

•

My mother miscarried twice before I was born and at least once after, which accounts for the large gaps in age between me and my sisters both older and younger. Her miscarriages preceded Kübler-Ross's naming of the five stages of grief. My mother had no language for what she knew in her body—that she had started to love these unborn, unnamed, and ultimately unburied children as they began to grow in her. The losses were visceral, wounding, more acute because they were not spoken of, not ritualized with religious services or casseroles brought to the house.

•

After two years of trying unsuccessfully to make a baby, my husband and I applied to adopt a child from Korea. We filled out paperwork and had our fingerprints run through a computer. A social worker asked us questions to determine our suitability as parents. Surprisingly soon, we were sent a passport-sized black and white photo of the girl who had been assigned to us.

A few months later, we waited at the gate with other anxious parents, pressed against the glass windows that looked onto the tarmac, shading our eyes to spot the jetliner traveling across space and time to bring our babies to us. I wasn't prepared for these other parents, for more than one baby to get off the plane. How would we know which one was ours? What if we got the wrong one? I wanted the little girl in the picture I'd been staring at for months. She hadn't come from my body, but I felt her in my bones.

•

I know about my mother's miscarriages from stories in which my father drives her, hemorrhaging, to the hospital. I didn't fully understand the impact of these losses until my daughter was grown. I spent a weekend at a family constellations workshop. Bert Hellinger, a German psychotherapist, developed the process, designed to heal unknown traumas and reveal family secrets that were passed down unconsciously from one generation to another. On my turn, I chose workshop participants to stand in for my father, my mother, and my siblings, intuitively positioning them in a silent tableau, each person like a star in a constellation deep in space.

The facilitator worked with the energy in the formation until a story took shape: children born and unborn. My mother, seated far across the circle, her head in her hands, weighed down with grief and the fear of more loss. My father, unable to move.

•

"Have you bonded yet?" I asked my husband every few weeks after our daughter arrived. "Have you?" he'd reply. It was our joke, to mask our anxiety. We needed to minimize, if not discredit, all the messages from child care books, his pregnant patients, and rude strangers in the grocery store that suggested tenuous and unsatisfactory parent-child relationships in the absence of natural childbirth and breastfeeding.

•

I was conceived shortly after one of my mother's miscarriages. Had that pregnancy gone to term, I would never have been born. The family constellation workshop showed my unborn sibling and me intertwined, one body wrapped around the other. Birth and death, love and loss, time and space.

•

I assumed my husband and I were not the only new adoptive parents who wondered how to build a family without genetic ties or a shared history, how to bond with a child whose face we gazed at without recognizing a familiar nose or eyes or even skin color, whose preverbal experiences were encrypted in ways we could not de-code, her DNA a mystery. I started a subscription-based newsletter where I could explore those questions for myself and for other adoptive parents.

In 1983, one year after the newsletter's birth, I bought one of the first personal computers, an IBM XT, with a Disk Operating System.

My husband and I carried the box downstairs to a room I'd designated as my office. I used a Swiss army knife to slice through the packing tape and carefully removed white Styrofoam from around the monitor that resembled a television with a picture tube. I held the box as my husband lifted the monitor onto my desk and connected it to the console containing the motherboard. I attached the keyboard, plugged it in, and stepped back the way I did when plugging in the Christmas tree lights.

"Do you think you'll really use that?" my husband asked as we waited for the "greater than" symbol to blink on the green screen.

"This is the future," I said.

•

I wrote about grief and loss. About the way infertility and adoption interrupt the circuitry that connects generations, about the weight of unfulfilled dreams and unspoken secrets for both parents and children. I wrote about how sorrow and joy don't comprise a calculation in which they are measured, computed, with a net result on the bottom line. Love and loss are intertwined, a symbiotic relationship. The existence of one doesn't cancel out the other.

•

The day my father died, I was answering essay questions in my theology class, the last final of my freshman year of college. I had reservations for a flight home immediately after the test.

The night before he died, the night before my last final, the night before my flight home for the summer, Mom called to say Dad had a stroke. Their bridge group was about to arrive. He was making old fashioneds. I was a thousand miles away. I couldn't get home any sooner than the flight I'd already booked, and my mother didn't want me to worry. She let me think he would recover, that his stroke was like the one my grandmother had years earlier, which left her right arm useless, her right foot dragging after her left. My mother didn't tell me a weak spot in my father's cerebral artery had given way, blood seeping into his brain like bitters into a sugar cube. She didn't tell me there wasn't anything they could do.

While my father took his last breaths, I was 35,000 feet above the Earth, imagining a future with him—the two of us watching television together, my father's left hand holding a cigarette, his right arm resting limply in his lap.

•

My freshman year of college, my father wrote me one letter, typing it on onionskin paper. My boyfriend and I were at colleges hundreds of miles apart. My father let me know he understood the suffering of this distance, let me know he liked this boy. I put the letter in the box where I kept the ones my boyfriend wrote to me, one every day we were apart.

After my father died, the distance between me and my boyfriend was too great—and by that I mean my father's loss was too great for me to carry alone. I transferred to the college my boyfriend went to. We graduated, we married, we made a family. I have all the letters we wrote that first year. I can't find the letter from my father.

•

The computer my father showed me that day in 1960 was designed to calculate trajectories of rocket ships. Time. Space. But for the anxious family members bravely looking up at the astronaut being launched into space, shading their eyes as the booster rocket disengaged from the main capsule in the early light of dawn like a teenager leaving for college, the computer was what they relied on to bring their loved one home.

The computer I use now weighs less than a newborn baby, sets in my lap. It is generations removed from the one my father showed me, but connects me to him across time and space.

Beyond Mt. St. Helens

Before

The rumbling went on for months—earth-shaking, steam-venting. Everyone on edge. The volcanologist on the mountain and the mother of a teenager who had crossed the line from adolescent angst to something deeper and more volatile both kept watch. They monitored signs, listened for subtle changes in the underground reverberations. And even though all the omens were there and they knew the cataclysm was possible, the day it happened, they weren't prepared.

·

The body of the scientist was never found.

Hundreds of miles east, the mother saw the dense black filling the sky in the west. She watched it move toward her. She said it was a thunderstorm that would soon pass.

Those don't look like thunderclouds, she thought.

She carried the storms of her Midwestern youth in her body—the feel of the south wind on her skin, the drop in barometric pressure in her chest. She sensed the approach of thunder and lightning unconsciously, the way she knew, even in her sleep, the slide of a bedroom window being opened, the sound of soft sneakers on the roof, the groan of tires rolling slowly across gravel.

It doesn't smell like rain.

Everything else seemed to be in order—traffic lights progressed from green to yellow to red, children held other mothers' hands as they crossed the street. But the advancing peril stretched across the sky in an unmistakable line. On one side, the cloudless blue of morning, the color of a baby's blanket and a child's eyes open in wonder; on the other, unbroken darkness.

No wind.
If this is a storm, there should be wind.

She watched the blackness pass overhead until it moved so far east it obliterated all the blue. The sun, too, disappeared in the middle of the day, eclipsed not by moon but by ash ejected from deep beneath the surface, the detritus of what had burned. The ash began to fall, deceptively soft, snow-like, disaster settling in slow motion. She could not deny what had happened: Explosion. White flows of hot gas. Molten rock. Magma. Melted glaciers. Splintered pines. Floods. Mud. Wasteland.

Screeching tires. Broken glass. Death.

Maybe you understand. Maybe you, too, told yourself it was a thunderstorm that would blow over. Maybe for you, denial ended when you saw the pills missing from the cabinet. Or perhaps you were the mother who drove, sleep-deprived, to the area under the bridge in the part of the city where you'd been told to look. Maybe you knew just before you saw fire flash from the barrel of the gun. Maybe you felt your bones shatter with the impact.

After

The mother went inside, shut the doors, closed the windows. She did not even answer the phone.

The ash—pulverized rock and volcanic glass—fell all day and into the real night, which she could no longer distinguish from day. Was it OK to breathe? The ash coated cars, peeled the paint the way a burn flays skin. Gray soot piled in the spaces between stalks of grain in wheat fields, heaped in streets, and became imprinted with the tracks of tires of those brave enough to leave their homes.

She was not brave.

Inside the house, stuffy with heat and blame, she longed for rain. Rain to cool the air, to restrain the powder that seeped into every opening, to wash it all away, to promise rebirth. When the rain came, it choked on the ash, changed it to sludge that filled the gutters, hardening as it dried. She tried to shovel it from the sidewalk, to clear a path for the children when they went back to school, but it was heavier than she could carry.

Some people scooped the muck into buckets, mixed it with stabilizers, spread it on plates and mugs and round bowls formed of clay, firing it until it was hard and glossy, transforming tragedy into art.

She was not a potter.

Maybe you heard about it or saw it on the news, and you said: *Couldn't she see the signs?*

She saw. She said it was a thunderstorm. Who expects eruption? Even the volcanologist's mother told herself he was probably safe.

Years Later

The mother breathes again without effort. She hikes the trail that meanders across hillsides still scarred moon-like from the blast. Some wounds never heal. But she sees growth too. New life. Huckleberry bushes with fat blue-red fruit. Fire moss. Noble fir. Beaded bone lichen. Sunflower.

Another path winds through green hummocks formed from landslides of mud and debris moving faster than highway speed limits. Alders grow straight. Elk calves live there now, a hopeful sign, though she knows they are vulnerable despite their size and the close eyes of mothers who would put their own bodies between them and danger.

At the Visitor's Center, the light in the room dims until there is only darkness. A video describes how theories of ecological regeneration have been affirmed and challenged by surprising stories of life overcoming catastrophe: Understory plants protected by a blanket of snow. Nutrients that rained from the sky—insects and pollen and seeds blown from the north and the south.

What survived was hit and miss. What grew was not predictable, didn't follow the steps experts outlined as required.

No one can promise resilience or redemption.
To some extent, recovery is a matter of chance.

Obstruction

Mom's hospital bed had been raised and the upper portion of the mattress angled so she seemed to be sitting slightly above the people gathered in her room to assess her mental competence. On one side of her bed stood interns and residents and physicians, all with stethoscopes draped around their necks, all wearing white lab coats with names embroidered in blue. They looked wooden—like folk carvings of doctors in different sizes, some with charts, some with their hands in their pockets.

Next to them stood the priest from Mom's church. Black pants. Short-sleeved black shirt. Roman collar. I invited him because Mom rarely made an important decision without consulting a priest. He showed up, which surprised me because he'd never visited Mom in her apartment a few blocks from the church.

I stood on the other side of Mom's bed, by the whiteboard where my name and phone number were written in a red marker that was so close to the end of its usefulness it barely streaked pink.

I was the daughter Mom had moved near when she decided she was ready for assisted living, the daughter with Mom's power of attorney for healthcare, the one the medical team had looked to for the past ten days because Mom was confused and hallucinating.

Until I made a decision they didn't like.

•

The patient is an eighty-nine-year-old woman who presented in the emergency room with abdominal discomfort. No immediate cause could be found, and she was admitted for observation. By morning she was breathing with difficulty and was largely unresponsive. When awakened she became agitated. A chest X-ray showed pneumonia.

Mom's pneumonia developed because she aspirated vomit while lying in the ER waiting to be seen. Like many elderly patients, she became confused and delirious just because she was in the hospital. Normally, Mom easily passed a mental status test.

Each month I took her to a psychiatrist who refilled her prescriptions for anxiety and depression and pain. Each time he asked Mom to draw a clock, name the president, repeat a sequence of words. She was anxious, depressed, and suffered arthritic feet, but her mind was still sharp. She read the inserts on the prescriptions I picked up for her at the pharmacy, examining the small type for signs of contraindications and side effects. She still subscribed to a daily newspaper, and we had thoughtful conversations about politics and current events as long as we avoided topics like abortion and stem cell research.

•

The day before Mom went to the ER, she stood in her living room leaning over her walker. She balanced on one hand while she swept her right arm from left to right like some octogenarian Vanna White.

"What am I doing here?" she asked me. "Is this any kind of life?"

Mom had outlived her husband, her siblings, and nearly all her friends. She found most of the other residents too demented for a decent game of bridge. She'd never watched much TV. Her days were long, often painful, but I'd never heard Mom question that God had a plan for her. I grew up hearing Mom tell me to meet disappointments and hardships by offering them up for the "poor souls in Purgatory," my suffering used to redeem their sins and release them to heaven. Our purpose on earth was outlined in the *Baltimore Catechism*, which, like every Catholic school student of my time, I knew by heart: "Our purpose is to know, love, and serve God in this world in order to gain the happiness of heaven."

As an adult, I'd embraced a different spiritual perspective, but Mom believed that by surrendering to the will of God she would one day attain the joy of eternal salvation. There she would be reunited with her loved ones—at least the believers. She wasn't sure about me. In recent years, her lifelong anxiety propelled her religiosity into scrupulosity. She reverted to some of the Catholic practices abandoned in the reforms of the 1960s, like fasting for hours before receiving communion. I wondered if she considered this an insurance policy.

For Mom to suggest that perhaps her life no longer had a purpose suggested not only an elderly person's existential crisis, but a crisis of faith.

I left Mom's apartment disturbed by her state of mind. Back home, the house felt heavy in the late afternoon heat of early August. The grass was brown and brittle. The sun shone defiantly above the basalt cliffs I could see from my deck, as though refusing to set. I changed into cycling shorts and put my bike on the rack of my car. I drove to the path by the river and cycled on the trail that climbed and dropped, requiring me to shift gears quickly. I watched for rocks that might have fallen from one of the ledges. I chose this path when I wanted to clear my head, a kind of meditation, the smell of pine and earth like incense. By the time I finished the twenty-five mile loop, the sun was starting to flag. I left my bike by the car and walked to the river, spent. I sat on a boulder drinking the last of my water, noticing the colored stones in the shallow spots of the river, and I talked to my father.

I didn't believe, as Mom did, that disembodied souls floated in Paradise, looking at the gate every time it opened to see if a loved one was there for a reunion. But I did believe in a spirit world, in souls.

"I don't want to mess with any Divine plans . . . " I said to Dad. I'd read a lot of fairy tales and was all too aware of the folly that awaited people who messed with fate—people who were granted three wishes and ended up with a pickle for a nose.

" . . . but I think it's time, and you need to help."

"Do something," I said to Dad. "I've been taking care of Mom for a long time, and now it's your turn." That wasn't exactly my spiritual belief, but it was my prayer. So I was surprised—and not surprised—when Mom woke the next morning with a stomachache severe enough to take her to the ER and within twenty-four hours was breathing with such difficulty that I called a priest to anoint her with Last Rites.

That night I slept in her hospital room, not wanting Mom to be alone if she died. I woke to the strange stillness of a hospital at night with a vague fear about what might have roused me. The light from the streetlamps outside filtered through the partially closed blinds forming pink stripes on the white sheets on my cot. I got up and looked at Mom. She was naked, her pale flesh streaked with blood. Her hospital gown was crumpled at the foot of her bed. Bloody tubes from her IVs lay on the floor. I heard her labored breathing—she had disconnected her oxygen too. I ran to get the nurse and stood in the hall while they cleaned Mom up and reconnected her to oxygen and antibiotics. I was grateful to have been there.

•

In the morning, the attending physician told me Mom's abdominal pain was due to a bowel obstruction. This is not another name for a particularly obstinate case of constipation, but a twisting or kinking of the bowel. Sometimes the intestine becomes entangled in post-operative scar tissue that can span the abdominal cavity like a spider web. Sometimes a mass, possibly undetectable in its early stage, presses on the bowel. The bowel cramps, causing severe pain. The stomach is unable to process food. Waste backs up. Nausea. Vomiting.

Tests didn't show what caused Mom's obstruction, but when the bowel is kinked or tangled in scars, it usually returns to its normal state after it's rested. It could take as long as a week. Mom would be given IV fluids to keep her hydrated, and a nasogastric tube would suck out her stomach contents along with the gases that built up there. If that didn't work, surgery might be needed.

The internist looked grim as he described that option. "Abdominal surgery on an eighty-nine-year-old woman is risky," he said. "The surgery itself might kill her." Even if successful, Mom might need a colostomy, in which the intestine is rerouted to an exit in the abdomen where it dumps feces into a bag. The post-operative recovery would be slow and unpleasant, requiring Mom to do a lot of rehab to regain her strength and mobility, which was declining even without the surgery.

Without the operation, Mom would be unable to process food and would starve to death.

The internist stood on the other side of Mom's hospital bed from me, his arms folded around Mom's chart. "You'll have a tough decision if it comes to that," he said, adding: "There's no right or wrong answer."

•

Mom had a living will, and we'd discussed end-of-life decisions candidly. The year before, when her doctor wanted Mom to have a mammogram, Mom shook her head no.

"I wouldn't have chemo anyway," she said, "so why get a mammogram?"

We disagreed when the news broke that Terri Schiavo's husband convinced a Florida judge to remove his wife's feeding tube after she'd been in a vegetative state for fifteen years. Mom understood why I would want my husband to do as Terri Schiavo's had, but the Catholic Church said that while no heroic measures need to be taken to extend life, no active action could be taken to hasten death. You didn't have to put in a feeding tube to save a life, but once it was in, you couldn't take it out. Mom trusted me to follow the Church's teachings regardless of my own feelings and beliefs.

But living wills are checklists, often filled out by a healthy person. There are questions about whether to resuscitate but none about how much suffering a person is willing to tolerate. There's no context for questions like: Do you want surgery if it is only to prolong life? What kind of surgery? What quality of life? Decisions about whether a person would want chemotherapy or heroic measures can be different in the abstract than when that choice is imminent.

Over the years, I'd talked with my husband, a family doctor, about the realities and ethics of end-of-life care. I remembered the time he'd arrived at the ER to find the staff drawing blood and connecting a ventilator to a woman who'd talked with him about her wishes, how he told the staff to stop, how he stayed with her and held her hand as she passed, knowing he could have gotten her a few more months, knowing she didn't want him to.

There were times, too, when he told me about families who clung to hope when there was none and who made decisions more from regret and fear than from compassion.

I knew the Church allowed someone to refuse surgery without considering it suicide, a mortal sin that would condemn the person to hell for all eternity.

But what would Mom choose if she could? I could be right that her questioning whether her life still had a purpose might mean she was ready to die, but did that mean she would refuse surgery? We don't always choose what we want or what's best for us.

I knew this decision was about what Mom would want, not what I wanted, but could I separate my belief that Mom had already come to the end of her life from the question of whether I should end it by refusing surgery?

It wasn't just Mom's statement the night before she became ill that had me thinking her work in this lifetime had been completed. A month before, my sister Ellen was visiting Mom in her assisted living apartment, ordering meals from the kitchen to be delivered, buzzing for the nurse's aide if she wanted a Tylenol. She slept beside Mom in her double bed, claiming that no other bed would work for her with her back pain, declaring a guest room in the facility was out of the question with her diabetes.

This was Ellen's third extended visit in the past year. During the first visit, Ellen fell and hit her head, requiring me to sleep on the couch to monitor her for a possible concussion. The ER staff carefully suggested "overmedication" was involved. On the second visit she told the head nurse that she was taking Mom home to live with her because I was abusing her—a claim the nurse dismissed as unfounded. One evening three weeks into Ellen's third visit, when Mom and I were alone, Mom put her head in her hands and when she lifted it, I saw her cheeks were wet.

"I want my bed back," Mom said. "I want my apartment back. I love Ellen, but this is too much."

I nodded.

"But I'm afraid if I tell her to go home, I'll never see her again."

Before this recent string of visits, it had been five years

since Mom had seen Ellen. Mom thought Ellen was punishing her for moving near me.

"You can't predict how Ellen will react," I said. "You have to be prepared for her to be mad."

"Will you tell her?" Mom asked. "Will you tell her she has to go home?"

"I will if you want me to, but I don't think she'll listen to me. It's your home. I think you have to do it."

When Ellen returned, Mom was caring and gentle, telling Ellen how much she loved her and enjoyed having her around, but that she needed her space.

Ellen smiled. "I'm not well enough to travel."

I shouldn't have been surprised at Ellen's response, at the convenience with which her physical ailments came and went, but I was.

Mom didn't hesitate. She reached for the phone and dialed Ellen's number. She told Ellen's husband that he needed to make plans to arrive the next day because Ellen couldn't travel alone.

Ellen left two days later, and Mom held her as though it would be the last time.

When I told my husband how Mom stood up to Ellen, he took a deep breath.

"Now Mom can die," he said.

I nodded in agreement.

Mom had spent much of her life afraid, looking to her father, my father, and the Church to make decisions for her. She had four daughters, all of whom were strong and independent—though not always in healthy ways—but she herself had struggled to find courage. She wanted to work but never challenged my father's preference that she stay at home. She suffered multiple miscarriages but never considered defying the Church's ban on birth control. She faced the challenges that came her way, but they left her sad and fearful. Her assertiveness with Ellen was deliberate risk-taking I hadn't seen in her. I believed she had fulfilled a task the universe had set for her.

In my spiritual system, this meant something.

So when I heard Mom question her purpose in living, I believed she was not just expressing fatigue at the daily struggle of life at eighty-nine, but was acting from a sense that she had learned what she was here to learn. She was done.

I forgot that the universe would want to make sure the lesson had been mastered. And I forgot that same universe was going to test me as well. I wasn't going to get a pickle for a nose, but I had poked at fate, and it wouldn't let me off easily.

.

Despite the rest Mom's bowel was given, it did not relax. The pneumonia improved, however, and Mom awakened for longer periods each day. She recognized me, but she was still confused. I didn't discuss her condition with her, and neither did the doctors. We could all see she wouldn't have understood.

There's no right or wrong answer.

I talked to my three sisters.

"Pull the plug, Lo," Ellen said. "Mom would want you to pull the plug."

I thanked her and hung up the phone. "There's not actually a plug," I said to no one. It hadn't been a deep or nuanced conversation, but I put a tick in the box beside Ellen's name.

My sister Peg didn't think major surgery was a good idea for someone's Mom's age. Peg was certain there had to be a less invasive, less risky way to resolve the problem. She held onto that idea even after she'd talked to the doctors herself.

"Maybe you should get a second opinion," Peg said.

My sister Theresa, much younger than the rest of us, grew up spending part of each holiday accompanying Mom to the nursing home where Mom's mother lived for years after a series of strokes. Grandma needed help with bathing and toileting and moving from the bed to a chair. "Mom said she never wanted to live like that," Theresa said when I called her.

We recalled Mom's inability to tolerate pain after a knee replacement ten years earlier, her resistance to participating in the physical therapy required, her anger when Theresa and I confronted her about the dependence she developed on pain medicine. Topics not on the living will.

"I'm not going to second guess you," Theresa said. "I'll back up whatever you decide."

I knew Mom would also want my husband to weigh in. She liked him and respected his medical expertise. He liked her. His own mother died a year after we were married, and he called my mother Mom. I told him I didn't think Mom would want the surgery—especially if the recovery proved difficult.

"The thing is, if she has the surgery, and it turns out well, I'll know I made the right decision, and if it goes badly, I'll know I made the wrong decision," I said. "But if she doesn't have the surgery, I'll never know if I did the right thing."

He took my hand.

"What do you think I should do?" I asked.

"I think you're making the right decision," he said. "But if it were me, I don't know if I could do it."

I arranged for a second opinion.

●

I was in my living room doing Sphinx Pose, lifting my torso while I rested on my forearms, when the surgeon called.

"I've seen your mother. I don't see any problems. I have her on my schedule for tomorrow."

I stood up, took a wide stance, turning my feet as though moving into Warrior Pose.

"There must be some misunderstanding," I said. "We were hoping you could give us an alternative to surgery."

"There is none. We do this all the time. We have good outcomes."

I knew surgeons were the cowboys of medicine, known for their need to fix problems and then ride off into the sunset. This surgeon did not see an elderly woman fearful of pain and an undignified descent into complete dependence. He did not see daughters who were bringing a shared understanding of their mother to their decision. He saw a surgical challenge, his responsibility only until the patient woke up from anesthesia. He would write the orders for rehab and pain meds and never see Mom again. If the surgery failed and the patient didn't wake up, well, she was eighty-nine years old; no one would fault him.

I shifted my weight, rotated my torso, bent one knee, ground my heels into the mat. Mentally, I gathered my clan around me, thinking of us as a tribe of indeterminate size and power. I spoke of us in the third person.

"This is the family's decision, and the family does not want surgery."

I expected him to be dismissive or argumentative, maybe even insulting. I was not prepared for what he said next:

"Then I'll go to court to get custody of your mother on grounds of elder abuse."

I hung up and dropped to the floor, folding into Child's Pose, my forehead resting on the yoga mat.

•

My husband suggested I speak to the medical ethicist, and I was surprised to hear there was such a person, surprised that no one had suggested that we talk.

The ethicist was a physician who'd been trained to see the big picture unobstructed by love and guilt and longing, trained in the nexus of compassion and practicality. She listened attentively as I recounted the conversations with the surgeon and with the attending who had told me there was no right or wrong answer. I shared my sisters' responses. I didn't mention my talk with my father or my mother's farewell to Ellen.

The ethicist sighed. "I'm the one who usually makes these points." She said she would support whatever decision we made and offered to talk to the surgeon, indicating in the subtle language of the medical community that he was a known bully.

She called me later that day. She'd talked to the surgeon. They did this surgery all the time. They had good outcomes. She'd also talked to Mom. "I think she might be able to make this decision herself," she said, and scheduled a meeting with Mom's medical team the following day.

That's how we came to be gathered around Mom in her elevated hospital bed. Her white hair was mussed and unwashed, but Mom nonetheless looked as though she was holding court. She smiled in a way that wasn't her, the way you do when you're supposed to know people and don't want to let on that you can't remember who they are.

·

I imagined the meeting would go something like this: First, someone would assess Mom's ability to make her own medical decisions. "Can you name the president? Can you draw a clock?" If Mom was deemed competent, someone would explain her diagnosis and its gravity. They would encourage her to take time to consider the treatment options. I knew that if Mom were "herself," she would ask questions and would want to talk it over with me, my sisters, and my husband. She would want to be sure that the options she was considering were sanctioned by the Church, that declining surgery was not a sin.

This was not how the meeting went.

The attending physician began by asking Mom if she knew why she was in the hospital. This was part two of my imagined scenario. There would be no part one; Mom's competence to make this decision was assumed.

Mom's smile broadened; she looked pleased that she knew the answer. "There's something wrong with my stomach." She nodded once. *So there. Ask me another question.*

"And do you remember what we talked about yesterday?" the attending asked.

The question took me by surprise. I didn't know anyone had discussed Mom's condition with her. I hadn't talked with her about it when I saw her the previous day. I didn't want to be accused of trying to influence her—hell, I didn't want to influence her. This was not a decision about whether Mom would have jello or pudding. I would take responsibility for the decision if I had to, and I would fight the medical establishment for my right to do so, if I had to. But I wouldn't fight Mom for it.

The attending leaned in. "Do you remember that we talked about how you need surgery or you will die?"

Mom nodded. "Oh, yes."

"And what do you remember about the surgery?"

Mom stopped smiling. She didn't know the answer.

There were no more questions requiring Mom to remember. No more questions that might stump her.

The attending leaned in. "You have to decide if you want to have surgery." This was a directive.

Mom's smile returned. She knew how to respond to authority. "Well," she said, with inappropriate gaiety, "I guess if I'm going to die without the surgery, I should have the surgery." *Or maybe I should have the pudding.*

Have surgery or die. Who wouldn't choose the jello?

I realized Mom was not going to ask for time to think about it or talk it over. I moved closer to her bed. "Mom, what do you remember being told yesterday about the recovery period after the surgery and what your life might be like?"

She looked at me, puzzled. The attending prompted her:

"You're going to need to be very committed to your rehab."

Mom looked coy at the mention of rehab. "Oh, I'm not very good with that," she said, sounding like a teenager on a first date who doesn't want to look smarter than the boy.

The priest took a step towards the bed. "We'll just have to come by and cheer you on." He pumped his fist, as though

Notre Dame just scored a touchdown. Mom brightened at the mention of regular visits from the priest.

The attending patted Mom's shoulder. "Well then, we'll get you on the schedule."

Everyone filed out of the room. The residents and intern and the priest quickly headed off to other duties. The attending and the ethicist stood at the nurses' station while the attending wrote the necessary orders. I walked up to them and cleared my throat.

"I see where this is going," I said, "and I'm not going to get in your way. But let's be honest. That was not 'informed consent.'"

The ethicist did not look at me. "You're right," she said. "But it's good enough for a surgeon."

I said I didn't want the operation performed by the surgeon who had threatened me, and she agreed.

I left the hospital. I sat in my car, which had been parked on the street in the August heat and was as stuffy as the attic of an old house. I slammed my fists on the steering wheel as I cried angry, cried sad, cried overwhelmed. Cried failure.

•

When I arrived at the hospital the following morning, the new surgeon was just coming out of Mom's room. He told me they did the operation all the time with good outcomes. He handed me a pen and a clipboard with a consent form.

I handed it back. "I'm not signing that." I didn't know how much he'd been told, but if the hospital's position was that Mom could decide on the surgery herself, they would have to own that decision. The surgeon walked back into Mom's room, and when he came out, he walked down the hall toward the elevators without a glance in my direction.

I went into Mom's room. She looked peaceful. She was fingering a rosary with blue glass beads and praying out loud. She stopped and rolled her head to face me.

"I'm going on a grand journey," she said. "I hope to see you all there someday."

64

Before I could respond, the orderly arrived, and with help from the nurse, moved Mom from her hospital bed to a gurney. I walked beside Mom as she was pushed to the elevator, my hand on hers and on the beads threaded through her fingers. Mom continued to say *Hail Marys* and *Our Fathers*. Her words became increasingly intense until she abandoned the ritual prayers and spoke spontaneously, her words bouncing off the metal walls of the elevator as we traveled down to the lowest level of the hospital:

"Take me now, Lord. Take me now."

I sighed. *So this is how it's going to go.* Mom didn't want to live but was unable to choose what she wanted. This was the test of her courage, and she was handing it over to God, the way she always had. I struggled with disappointment and sadness, but I leaned over her and whispered close to her ear: "Mom, if at any time you want to just let go, it's OK."

The elevator stopped. The doors opened to the pre-op room. Pink and beige tiles covered the floor and walls of a room that could easily have been designed as a school cafeteria. Light streamed in from high windows. It smelled chemically clean. People in scrubs moved quickly in and out of patient areas that were defined by curtains. I recognized the surgeon who'd asked me to sign the consent. The orderly pushed Mom into one of the stations.

A tall man, his surgical mask hanging around his neck, pulled back the curtain and introduced himself as the anesthesiologist. He asked Mom her name. Her date of birth. Why she was there. He told her what to expect from the anesthesia. He stepped out to talk to a nurse, leaving open the curtain.

After a few moments, without moving, without preamble, Mom spoke: "I'm not sure I want to do this."

I saw the anesthesiologist straighten, stop what he was doing. I knew he heard.

"I think I made this decision for the wrong reasons," Mom said. "I don't think this is what I want."

The anesthesiologist took two strides to reach Mom's bedside. "Do you have any questions I can help you with?"

Mom rolled onto her back to look at him. "I'm having doubts. I think I've allowed myself to be talked into this. I don't think this is the will of God. I want to stop this." The anesthesiologist looked at me and jerked his head, motioning me to follow him. We stepped outside the curtain. He drew it shut.

"We do this surgery all the time," he said. "We have good results. We can do this."

This was not news to me, and now it was also beside the point.

"You're talking to the wrong person."

He looked at me, confused. "You're the healthcare proxy, right?"

"I am. But I didn't sign the consent."

"She signed?" he asked, surprised.

He stood up even straighter than before, into the stance of someone who is about to make an important pronouncement.

"Then, ethically, I can't proceed."

He called the surgeon over.

"I do not want this surgery," Mom said to him.

I closed my eyes and let out a breath.

•

Mom died a week later. In that week I came to understand that death does not always arrive in an instant—one minute you're fully alive, and the next minute you're dead. During her time in hospice, Mom occupied a liminal space between life and death, and in some ways, I stepped into it with her. I think we'd actually stepped into it weeks before.

If the hospital was a place of action and antiseptic, the hospice facility radiated peace: wood beams, spacious rooms that opened to a grassy courtyard, the oniony smell of soup always warming on the stove in the kitchen, the earthy fragrance of fresh coffee. No one rushed. I rolled out my yoga mat in a chapel with a wall of glass revealing a garden of stones and ferns. I moved through Sun Salute.

Mom seemed comfortable and slept most of the time, but one afternoon she opened her eyes when I entered the room. She smiled and lifted her head from the pillow.

"Oh, Lois," she said. "How beautiful you are."

I'd been under stress for weeks. My mother was dying. I did not look beautiful. But I sensed Mom was not looking *at* me, but *through* me to something beyond.

I walked over to the foot of the bed, not fishing for a compliment but curious to hear more. "Tell me what you see."

"An angel. You look like an angel." She leaned her head back on the pillow, nearly rapturous. "Oh, I am so happy."

Whatever Mom saw, it seemed to give her reassurance. She was going on a grand journey. She would be reunited with *all* her loved ones. There would be angels.

That was not my spiritual belief, but it was my prayer for her.

Mom said she'd like something to eat. A brochure I'd been given said that sudden alertness and hunger were paradoxical signs of entry into the last stages of dying.

"What would you like?" I actually offered jello and pudding.

"I'd like one of those French dip sandwiches from Quizno's." It had been her go-to lunch when I would take her shopping or to the doctor's office.

She'd lost her appetite by the time I returned with the sandwich. I unwrapped it and broke off a bit of the bun. I dipped it in the small plastic tub of roast beef juice. She opened her mouth, and I placed the soaked bread on her tongue.

WORK

Bread and Roses

Yes, her hands may be hardened from labor
And her dress may not be very fine
But a heart in her bosom is beating
That is true to her class and her kind

— Joe Hill, "The Rebel Girl" (in honor of
Elizabeth Gurley Flynn), 1911

I met Sol, an organizer for the International Typographical Union (ITU), in the lobby of the Howard Johnson's where he'd taken a room. Outside, the uniform Indiana landscape stretched unbroken to the horizon, fields of corn made square by roads laid out in a grid. Humidity made my cotton T-shirt stick to my back, and I shivered slightly from the sudden cool of the hotel lobby and the risk of what I was about to do.

Sol was short and stocky with a creviced face and thick, stubby fingers. He wasn't the first union organizer I'd met. As a newspaper reporter, I'd interviewed the founder of the Farm Laborers' Organizing Committee, who was doing for Midwest farm workers what Cesar Chavez was doing in California. But

I hadn't called Sol for an interview; I called to ask him to help me start a union at the newspaper.

I didn't think I looked the part of a labor activist. I wore polyester blouses with a bow at the throat—I didn't call them "pussy bows" in 1978—skirts I made myself, platform shoes with three-inch heels. I had soft hands, smooth skin, blue eye shadow. My hair smelled like Breck shampoo. I didn't know then of the many women who'd built the labor movement in the United States, women who often were also journalists as well as suffragists and who took far greater risks when they spoke out than I would.

I was twenty-five years old with a master's degree when, one year before I called Sol at the ITU, I was hired by the Muncie (Indiana) *Star*. I was the second woman hired at the paper to cover beats other than what was called "women's news"—weddings, food, and light features. The stories I wrote might expose corruption in county officials, generate an outpouring of support for a family left homeless by a fire, or whip up concern about a nuclear power plant. But within the structure of the newspaper itself I felt impotent and not only because I was a woman. The same family owned both the morning and evening newspapers. Anyone who wanted to work as a reporter in that town worked for Jim Quayle and the salary he offered. But workers don't come together to bargain just for economic reasons, I learned. They join with peers to demand the dignity and power that comes with the collective voice a union provides.

•

In the nineteenth century and into the twentieth, working women wore simple white cotton blouses with rounded collars, fastened up the back with buttons that dotted their vertebrae as they bent over desks in offices or stood up straight while writing on chalkboards in the front of classrooms. Though modeled after men's dress shirts, the women's version tapered at the waist—to show off the woman's form—and was tucked into a long skirt. The blouses were mass-produced in factories where their affordability was built on the backs of other women who bent over sewing machines, often for twelve to fourteen hours a day.

Though women in the labor force had little power, the shirtwaist nonetheless became a symbol of freedom, of women's movement out of domestic roles. Eventually suffragists added a matching white skirt, and this became the uniform of those marching for the right to vote. In November 2016, women voting for Hillary Clinton for president went to polling places wearing white to honor these suffragists. They wore pantsuits to follow Clinton's defiant resistance to wearing dresses and skirts. And in January 2017, they marched for dignity and power.

•

If I'd lived in the early nineteenth century, I likely would have been too privileged to be among the many young women who moved to cities from rural areas to find jobs in factories.

When I graduated from college in 1973, I was twenty-two and had never held a job of any kind. Other girls waited tables at Garfield's and sold blouses at Carlisle's department store, jobs that kept them on their feet for hours and paid far less than the jobs my boyfriend and his buddies could get.

Other than an uncle who was a bricklayer, no one in my family ever belonged to a union. I came from thinkers who explored ideas and solved problems. Soft bodies. Firm beliefs. I grew up believing that education was the portal to knowing what was right, and being right would give me power and garner respect. I got that idea from my father—a white, male mechanical engineer. So instead of slinging hash, I spent my college summers dissecting a fetal pig, conjugating Spanish verbs, carefully measuring liquids in graduated cylinders with my clear blue eyes protected by safety goggles.

•

The Lowell, Massachusetts, mills that dotted the canals of the Merrimack River were powered by energy produced by a stone dam above the Pawtucket Falls. Women and girls—initially from the New England countryside—worked in factory rooms where particles of thread and fabric speckled the air they breathed. The windows were kept closed to keep the humidity high, the fibers moist. The noise of the machines was a cacophony of spindles, rollers, and carriages pulling and weaving threads, harsh and deafening. After work the women walked to nearby boardinghouses to eat and sleep, grateful for the few minutes they could breathe fresh air, filling their lungs with the freshness of honeysuckle or snow.

In 1836, Harriet Hanson was eleven years old and worked as a "doffer," racing between the spinning frames with a large bobbin box, trying to be fast enough so the spinning frames barely stopped as she removed and replaced bobbins. In her 1898 autobiography, *Loom and Spindle, or Life among the Early Mill Girls,* she described how the workers responded to a cut in wages by organizing the "Factory Girls' Association" and deciding to "turn out." But when the day came and the girls on the upper floors walked out, those in the lower rooms, where Hanson worked, weren't sure whether to follow. I picture the flurry of activity coming to a halt, the factory becoming eerily silent as heads turned to see who would stay and who would go, then this eleven-year-old girl declaring her intention to strike and courageously walking out. I see her turn her head to look behind her and the wonder on her face when she sees the other girls lined up to follow her. I watch some 1,500 march out of the factory, one of the first strikes for better wages in the United States.

The workers walked to a nearby knoll and stood among the white birch and elms, whose leaves glistened like translucent gold coins on that October day, until one of the girls mounted the limestone trough of a pump and voiced their grievances.

She was the first woman to speak in public in Lowell, and I wonder if she was tentative at first, voice high and shaky as mine is when I try to speak about injustice. I try to imagine what it felt like for women who had never spoken out or walked out or defied authority in any way to feel they had power in their bodies. I think it felt like humming in their chests.

•

In my first job after college, I advanced quickly from an entry-level position writing press releases to acting chief of the news bureau at a state agency. The "acting" part of my title meant I had all the responsibilities but not the salary that went with the promotion; I didn't have the required experience for that pay grade. On business trips out of town, "acting" meant I also was expected to pretend to be my boss's girlfriend in public, sitting by him in restaurants and laughing at his stories.

I thought that by doing the job, I could add threads to the tapestry of the resume I was constructing. I thought my abilities would be noticed and rewarded, but I learned that you don't gain respect by working for less than you're worth. You don't have power if you're afraid you'll lose your job if you object to your boss flirting with you in public.

•

The labor movement was fostered by skilled workers who knew there was dignity in what they produced with their bodies. Typesetters were among the first to unionize.

Typography is the art of seamlessly arranging letters and words and spaces for publication. Typesetters selected a cast metal "sort" of a particular font or style and point size, keeping in mind that what they saw on the face was a mirror image of how the letter would appear on the printed page—they needed

75

to be able to mind their "p's" and "q's." They had to know how to read and spell. They needed an artistic yet analytical eye for the alignment and spacing of the letters and lines so that the page was visually attractive—leaving less space between tall, narrow letters like "i" and "l" than between rounded letters. All this, plus the manual dexterity to manipulate the sorts. It was good work for women, but women were not allowed to join the union.

•

My next job was writing press releases for women's sports teams at Ball State University. I hand-carried the pages to the Muncie *Star* where I begged the sports editor to find room for them. I remember him looking at a photo of a gymnast skimming over the uneven parallel bars and tossing it back at me, saying her outstretched legs were unsuitable for a family newspaper.

In 1976, Title IX had been passed but not yet implemented, and the women's teams were under-funded, patched together with remnants of used equipment and outdated facilities discarded by men. The athletes were driven not by the status or money they might achieve but by the longing of their bodies, lats and pecs and quads contracting, responding when asked to go longer, faster, harder.

Unlike the men's sports arenas that vibrated with the sounds of pep bands and cheerleaders and feet stomping the bleachers, the women's gymnasiums were dark with a few benches that were nonetheless more than adequate for the friends and parents who came to watch. The airless locker rooms held the dank smell of women's sweat, layered with traces of mildew and resentment.

The men ignored us. The women had their own governing body—the NCAA paid no attention then to teams that couldn't generate ticket sales or TV ratings. Because the salaries weren't sufficient to attract men, most coaches were women. I reported to the Women's Athletic Director (AD) in an organizational structure that paralleled the men's without intersecting.

The Women's AD took me with her to Indianapolis to vote for representatives to the 1977 International Women's Year conference. It was my first action in support of the women's movement. I'd been unaware of the thousands of women who marched in August of 1970 in the Women's Strike for Equality. My most radical feminist action in college had been to declare, in solidarity with the other women who staffed our college newspaper, that I would never write "women's news." Since women were considered too fragile to be exposed to the crimes and accidents they might cover as reporters, it was a more defiant statement than it may sound today—and also explains why I was writing press releases.

The conference was organized to identify goals for the progress of women. It had no authority to muscle those goals into reality, but giving them voice was sufficiently powerful to threaten those who opposed ratification of the Equal Rights Amendment and objected to women controlling their own bodies. Fundamentalist Christian churches bused their congregations to counter votes by feminists. The AD and I stood for four hours to cast our ballots, shifting our weight from one foot to the other as the day wore on. As activism goes, standing in line inside an air-conditioned convention center is tame. We didn't face police in riot gear, dogs or fire hoses, the National Guard. But I had a good view of the pastors—bible-thumping men—as they walked back and forth next to their flock, patrolling them with reminders of the candidates they said best represented women's interests. Despite the cool air, the ministers wiped dripping brows with linen handkerchiefs pulled from the breast pockets of their cheap, ill-fitting jackets sewn by women in sweatshops somewhere. I could see they were afraid that if the women weren't repeatedly told for whom they were to vote, they might make another choice, experience the power of their voice, and feel the humming of their defiant bodies, as I did that day.

That summer the university implemented Title IX by stitching together the men's and women's athletic departments in a way that moved all the women's positions into the organizational chart of the men's athletic department, like fingers from one hand slipping into the fingers of another. Each woman—including the AD—became organizationally subservient to the man who held the comparable title. I would become the Assistant Sports Information Director (SID) for Women, no longer reporting to the Women's AD but to the Men's SID. The Women's AD would report to the Men's AD, not to the administrator they'd both reported to previously. When I asked the Women's AD why she agreed to it, she said it gave her a seat at the table. I didn't say anything, but I knew it wasn't our table anymore and that power is not located in a seat but in a body with a voice and a chest that whirrs like a sewing machine.

•

Throughout nineteenth-century America, educated women might become teachers, and a few entered male-dominated fields like medicine and journalism. But few opportunities existed for women who looked at their world and had a vision for making it better—those we call leaders.

Augusta Lewis was eighteen when she became a newspaper reporter in 1866. She was fascinated by typesetting, and after apprenticing, joined the staff of the *New York World*. When the ITU struck in 1867, the women typesetters crossed picket lines. They were fired when the strike was settled. Lewis started the Women's Typographical Union. A few years later, with men torn between a desire to keep women out of the unions and the need to prevent them from becoming scabs, the ITU began admitting women, and Lewis was elected secretary. She married a fellow labor activist and started a newspaper to support women's suffrage.

•

Even before the men's and women's athletic departments at Ball State merged, the Men's SID tried to tell me how to do my job. I knew he had no authority to summon me to his office to review my work and that he wasn't serious about mentoring me. I also found his advice useless, like his suggestion that I use different colored paper for each sport—blue for basketball, yellow for soccer, green for golf. I wanted to ignore him, but my AD told me to act like I was listening, then do what I wanted. Pretend I respected him. Pretend he had authority over me. Make nice. She was my boss, so I went to his office when summoned and stood by his desk while I felt a slow burn in my gut.

I remembered when I was a junior at a high school that had no sports teams for girls. A sophomore who was a talented tennis player wasn't allowed to join the boys' team because she was too good. School officials feared the boys would feel demoralized if a girl beat them. Later that year, a friend and I were prohibited from running for president and vice president of Student Council because girls weren't allowed to hold those offices. Looking back, I'm more saddened than surprised that I didn't speak up or lead the other girls in a protest. I had less courage than an eleven-year-old doffer in a nineteenth-century mill. I wonder how my life would have changed if, at seventeen, I'd felt the power of my body walking out, marching, resisting.

·

By the twentieth century, garment workers were mostly women immigrants. Unions had more difficulty organizing them because sweatshops were isolated in tenements and workers spoke dozens of languages. Nonetheless, in 1909, a walkout by women at the Triangle Shirtwaist Factory was joined by 20,000 women in the garment industry. Still, conditions didn't improve. Two years later, fire broke out in a rag bin on the eighth floor of the factory in Greenwich

Village. Maybe it was a careless cigarette. Maybe a spark from one of the machines. Some doors and fire escapes were locked to prevent workers from stealing or taking unauthorized breaks. Only one elevator was working. As thick black smoke filled the rooms on the eighth, ninth, and tenth floors, panicked women ran from one locked door to another, covered their faces with fabric that moments before, they'd been making into dresses. They coughed as the heat became oppressive. Their lungs burned as they breathed in smoke. One of the few fire escapes collapsed from the weight of the first workers to flee, leaving the others stranded. Ladders from the fire engines only reached to the seventh floor.

Frances Perkins, a graduate student at Columbia, was having tea nearby when she heard the sirens. She ran to the scene to see some of the women leaping from windows, holding hands. The death toll was 146. The experience moved Perkins to work to improve working conditions for women and children, and later she became the Secretary of Labor, the first woman to hold a Cabinet position.

After the fire, the garment workers formed the International Ladies Garment Workers Union. The ILGWU label was sewn into every blouse I wore growing up, and during the time I was a reporter for the Muncie *Star*, the union advertised on prime-time television, their jingle an anthem for what made America great.

•

August 1977, just weeks from the start of the school year and fall sports. My mind was a chatter of injustices as I considered the re-organized athletic department and the irony that it was the implementation of Title IX that caused a loss of dignity and power. My husband and I were vacationing in Montana. He pulled off I-90 and into a gas station in a town north of Missoula, where the St. Regis River meets the Clark

Fork. A few yellow pine trees edged the parking lot I walked across to get to the phone booth. The air was hot and dry, the sky cloudless and the same blue as the lupine that edged the hillsides. My sleeveless white cotton blouse billowed in the wind. I pulled my blond hair off my face as eighteen-wheelers drove past, their diesel engines sounding like water in the turbines of a dam. I dropped coins into the pay phone, waiting for the clink of each one before inserting the next. I made two phone calls: the first to the AD to tell her I wouldn't be returning in the fall, and the second to the newspaper to apply for a job as a reporter.

•

The editor of the Muncie *Star* leaned back in his chair. He'd just offered me the job. I'd expressed some disappointment at the salary, which was even less than I'd made in the financially neglected Women's Athletic Department, my voice shaky, betraying my lack of skill in declaring my worth. "We're not a union shop," he said. "We give raises based on merit." It was a misleading statement about unions but the right button to push for me. I was accustomed to overachieving, to having to be twice as good to be considered half as qualified, and all that. At the newspaper, I thought, I wouldn't be held back because I didn't have the years a civil service job required for a pay grade or be limited by the budget allocated to women's sports. I'm sure my chest puffed a little with the thought of how quickly I'd be able to justify a merit raise.

Every night, I wrote my stories on an electric typewriter that purred with the speed of someone who'd learned to type so that she had a skill she could "fall back on." When the city editor asked who had something for the front page, I spun my chair around and pitched whatever I had—a rape trial, teacher negotiations, utility rate hike. More often than not, the editor nodded agreement. I'd give him the finished story, typed on newsprint that came on a spool. He marked up the copy and rolled it into a container that was sucked into a pneumatic tube and bulleted to the third floor where typesetters, no longer working with metal, turned it into narrow columns of glossy paper to be waxed into place. As our deadline approached, I often stood beside them, taking in their smell of cigarettes and ink, to approve cuts that would allow the columns to come out even.

When my work was done, I hung around the newsroom, reading wire copy or working on a feature story until I saw someone else ready to leave. The newspaper charged us to park in the lot adjacent to the building and I couldn't afford it. I parked blocks away, on the street, which was often deserted when I left at 11 P.M., or sometimes after midnight. I didn't want to walk to my car alone, but I didn't want to remind anyone that as a woman, I felt vulnerable.

Late one election night, I walked through downtown, stopping at Democratic headquarters before heading to Republican headquarters to gather reactions to the results. One candidate, an incumbent who'd unexpectedly lost, couldn't be found, but as I headed back to the newspaper, I spotted his campaign manager. "I'll take you to him," he said, and led me to a downtown hotel. I stepped into the elevator after him, my heels clicking, my heart beating fast as I wondered whether I was doing something I'd regret, yet believing that this was how women showed they could do the same job that men could do. I got the quote. But I couldn't tell anyone what I'd risked without reminding them that this kind of hazard was what had justified keeping women out of reporting jobs.

•

In 1905, Lucy Gonzalez Parsons told the International Workers of the World (IWW): "The trouble with all the strikes in the past has been this: the workingmen . . . strike and go out and starve. Their children starve. Their wives get discouraged. Some feel that they have to go out and beg for relief, and to get a little coal to keep the children warm, or a little bread to keep the wife from starving, or a little something to keep the spark of life in them so that they can remain wage slaves . . . My conception of the strike of the future is not to strike and go out and starve, but to strike and remain in and take possession of the necessary property of production."

Every sit-in at lunch counters in the Civil Rights movement, every teach-in during the anti-war movement, every tent set up during the Arab Spring and the Occupy movement reverberated with the voice of Lucy Gonzalez Parsons advocating for a new form of workplace activism. I've talked to people who lived in the Occupy camps, heard them say that what started as a message to the world about how we could live more communally and more compassionately took hold in their bodies during the days they lived the idea. They came together with people who had been strangers to eat, listen to each others' stories, stand up together when the police came to clear the camps. Something shifted, they told me, and it stayed with them even after the tents were torn down, the protest dispersed.

In 1905, Parsons and "Mother" Jones were the only women delegates at the founding convention of the International Workers of the World—known as the Wobblies—which welcomed everyone, including women, African Americans, and immigrants. Parsons was the only woman to speak.

Born a slave and claiming Mexican, Native American, and African heritage, Parsons and her white husband moved to Chicago where they became anarchists and socialists and activists in the labor movement. I picture her and Albert with their two children, Albert Jr. and Lulu, marching at the head of some 80,000 workers in the world's first May Day parade in 1886, demanding an eight-hour work day and justice for workers locked out of the McCormick Harvester plant. Clandestine meetings in tenement flats. Inked fingers from printing presses turning out underground newspapers like *The Alarm* with Parsons's essays advocating that activists learn how to use sabotage and explosives.

Parsons was a feminist who wasn't a suffragist because she wanted to smash the state, not find a way to live in it. I imagine her chest bombinating when the Chicago police called her "more dangerous than a thousand rioters."

•

As a reporter, I could sense when a county official underestimated me because I was young and small and a woman, and I didn't hesitate to use that to my advantage, asking the softball questions they expected until their guard was down, then hitting them with a hard one. One day I walked into the office of an agency spokesman who hadn't looked good in the last story I wrote. He frowned, leaned in close, and jabbed the air with his index finger inches from my rib cage: "You come in here with your blouse and that bow at your neck, looking all soft, and then you fucking break both my thumbs," he said. I raised an eyebrow.

The day after a blizzard shut down most of the Midwest, the wind blowing snow across the flat until it drifted so high that when I opened my garage door from the inside I couldn't see over the wall of white, the newspaper's photographer drove a snowmobile to the duplex where I lived to bring me to work. A skeleton crew put together the paper, working in a building with no heat, me typing in wool gloves with the fingertips cut off. Snow would block the trucks needed to distribute the newspapers—they would remain on the loading dock—but it was important to the management of a daily newspaper that they not miss a day of publication.

Believing I'd proved my worth, I walked into the editor's office and asked for a raise. The editor didn't even look up from the copy he was reading when he told me I'd get an annual raise when everyone else did—a different message than I'd been given when I was hired.

It was my Norma Rae moment. I didn't stand on a desk with a sign that said STRIKE, but it was the moment when I knew that I couldn't just quit when I was being fucked over and try to find another job where I wouldn't be. Those jobs didn't exist.

Rosabeth Moss Kanter's study of men and women in corporations was published the year I started working at the *Star*, although I didn't read it for another thirty years. Women who didn't accept male "protection" in organizations were ostracized, and other women didn't support them out of fear of being ostracized. Neither was a path to power. She concluded that for individual women to have power in organizations, they needed sufficient numbers. That wasn't true in the garment factories, and we know now that more women doesn't necessarily mean more power. In 1978, what I knew was that one path to power in an organization was a union. When I called unions, they told me that it wasn't enough to organize the reporters, we needed to be able to silence the printing presses too. We needed to be able to shut down the newspaper.

•

If I had been one of the theater-goers emerging from the Gaiety or any of the other theaters in Times Square one night in 1906, I would have seen a delicate sixteen-year-old standing on a makeshift stage lit by red flares. I might have walked past in an effort to get to a lobster palace where their sumptuous meal might be interrupted by an announcement that Lillian Russell, Diamond Jim Brady, or Florenz Ziegfeld had just arrived. But I think I would have been one of those who stopped to listen, intrigued by the sight of Elizabeth Gurley Flynn. Reports say she wore a schoolgirl's dress, her dark hair in braids that hung down her back, her eyes clear and blue. I likely would have found myself frowning when she frowned, laughing when she laughed, captured by the oratorical skills that would mesmerize audiences for the rest of Flynn's public life as she declared: "Workers must unite to destroy capitalism." I might have stood in shock as she was arrested for speaking out.

Drawn by a militancy that she felt lacking in the "stodgy" Socialist Party of her parents, Flynn left school to join the IWW. During her life, she would organize garment workers in Pennsylvania, silk weavers in New Jersey, restaurant workers in New York, miners in Minnesota. She would chain herself to a lamppost in Spokane in a campaign for free speech, advocate for women's rights, help start the ACLU, and be jailed during the McCarthy era. She turned sixty-five and then sixty-six at the federal women's prison in Alderson, West Virginia, for advocating the overthrow of the government.

Photographs of her as an adult show her wearing a white shirtwaist blouse with a plaid bow at the neck, standing on a soap box, leaning forward with one arm raised to emphasize her point. Involuntarily, I lean in as though I'll be able hear what she's saying.

•

One day in January 1912, the weaving room in one of the woolen mills in Lawrence, Massachusetts, became silent as women spontaneously abandoned the power looms that clattered ten hours a day. By the following day, the strike had spread to the other mills. Workers shouted for those still on the job to strike. They slashed thread and bolts of cloth and belts on machines, tore bobbins and shuttles off looms. Outside the red brick factories, snow fell as workers shattered windows with bricks and ice and police swung at them with billy clubs. More than 10,000 women who wove wool into coats shivered in the crisp New England air as they walked picket lines, unable to afford warm coats of their own. One morning the police drenched the women with water from fire hoses. The mayor called in the militia who pointed bayonets at the women who sang as they marched. Their voices were lifted by the movement of their diaphragms and their feet and the knowledge that together they could bring the mill owners to their knees.

Inadequate wages. Sixty-hour work weeks. Unsanitary drinking water. Child labor. Machines that maimed and killed. Ethnic slurs. Sexual harassment. A life expectancy twenty years less than average.

The women were Polish, Hungarian, Slavic, and Syrian immigrants, some of whom had been enticed to come to America after seeing posters of workers walking out of the mills with bags of money under their arms. They spoke forty-five different languages, couldn't vote, weren't citizens. The strike was sparked by a cut in hours that meant less pay, but the workers did not only want food; they wanted working conditions that left them able to enjoy nature, relationships, and their time away from the mill. It became known as the Bread and Roses Strike, referencing a phrase coined by suffragist Helen Todd in 1920.

Elizabeth Gurley Flynn was one of the IWW organizers who went to Lawrence.

When the mill owners brought in scabs, the striking workers attacked streetcars carrying them. The militia beat the strikers with batons and the ends of their rifles. One woman was shot and killed. The workers suspected the militia, but some of the IWW organizers were arrested and charged with murder and inciting a riot, leaving Flynn to lead the resistance.

Flynn knew how to speak to immigrants with the kind of English that their school-age children used when speaking to their parents at home—simple words, short sentences. As she had when she stood on a soap box in Times Square, she ignited a spirit in the crowd, stirred them.

As the strike wore on, Flynn organized the evacuation of children to the homes of socialists in other cities. The publicity when thousands met the first train at Grand Central Station prompted officials to order the next group of mothers who gathered at a train station to disperse. The mothers defied the order, hastily lifting their children into the waiting cars, determined to send them to safety. The police responded by beating the women, dragging them by the hair, and arresting them. One had a miscarriage. The nation was outraged. The mill settled. The gains the workers made were soon eroded again, but the women felt the power of bodies moving together as it surged in their chests.

•

Women organized workers in other industries too: Agnes Nestor, glove makers; Clara Lemlich, shirtwaist makers; Fannie Sellins, coal miners; Emma Terayuca, pecan shellers; Luisa Moreno, cannery workers; Velma Hopkins, tobacco workers; and Jessie de la Cruz, farm workers.

I didn't know any of this history when I called the ITU and asked them to send an organizer. Learning it now, it makes sense that women who could weave the lived experiences of women into an articulate vision of a world in which they were treated with dignity would gravitate to leadership roles in the labor movement. I am not surprised that many of them were also suffragists and journalists and left autobiographical accounts bearing witness. They were women who had found their voices by putting their bodies at risk.

I don't put myself in the company of women who had to choose between exhaustion and starvation, nor of those who faced being beaten or jailed for speaking up. I had no children to feed. I had a husband who was employed. We struggled as young couples do, but we knew we had a future that didn't depend on my publisher treating me fairly. I was born privileged, and I expected to be treated with dignity. In 1978, I saw empty promises, lack of recognition, and my own powerlessness through the lens of the women's movement that peaked as I came of age.

The newspaper wasn't a turn-of-the-century sweatshop that locked us in to keep us from stealing. But single reporters couldn't afford rent on their own, even in a small working class town in Indiana. Some couldn't afford telephones. We deserved higher wages, yes, but we also deserved dignity. Bread and roses. The moment I knew the editor had lied to me, I knew he didn't respect me.

Sol was clear about what I could expect if we organized a union. "Management will say you are lazy. They'll say you're a freeloader, a trouble-maker; that you've always been a problem." I couldn't imagine anyone saying that about me, a good Catholic girl who had a front page story nearly every day and a bow on my blouse, so I said I wasn't worried.

In Sol's motel room, I called two other reporters who joined us within minutes. We called some typesetters, and by the end of the night we had an organizing committee and a draft of a letter informing the publisher of our intention to form a union. The fluttering in my stomach that I'd felt since I called the ITU began to move up, into my chest.

•

Rose Pesotta was one of several union leaders who graduated from Bryn Mawr's Summer School for Women Workers, which began in 1921 to educate women factory workers in the liberal arts using a progressive approach that included classroom discussion. The programs spread—some limited to women and some co-educational: Barnard College, University of Wisconsin, Sweet Briar College, Occidental College, University of California, Berkeley.

Pesotta was a Russian Ukranian Jew, an immigrant who started as a seamstress in a shirtwaist factory and eventually was blacklisted for organizing workers in Puerto Rico, Detroit, Montreal, Cleveland, Buffalo, Boston, Salt Lake City, and Los Angeles. The International Ladies Garment Workers Union elected her vice president in 1934, but she refused a fourth term in 1944 because she was still the only female officer. "One woman vice president could not adequately represent the women who now make up 85 percent of the International's membership of 305,000," she said.

Pesotta was an exception; more often, women's leadership in the labor and suffrage movements was informal, not based in the authority of organizational position but in the power of voices that let workers and women know someone understood them.

Mary Field Belenky and her colleagues described how women who were disconnected from their voices by poverty, culture, lack of education, or abuse developed self-awareness and self-confidence by learning how to listen to their own experience, questioning authority, and weaving multiple sources of knowledge together without losing the thread of their own stories. Belenky called this "women's ways of knowing," but I think of it as self-empowerment, as leadership development, as what seamstresses and glove makers did as they talked about their day while they ate a slice of bread during their lunch break or walked back to boarding houses from factories and mills and later heard those experiences re-framed by women like Elizabeth Gurley Flynn and Lucy Parsons and Rose Pesotta.

•

Sol, of course, was right. Management maligned us, sending letters describing the organizing committee as shiftless, wanting something for nothing. Reporters not on the organizing committee were suddenly offered salary increases and promotions—enticements that were considered unfair labor practices, designed to convince workers that management didn't need a union to respond to grievances. One night I awoke to the tinkle of glass breaking. In the morning I found a red brick in the back seat of my car, resting on jagged pieces of my rear window. I felt my heart pounding, the beats echoing with those of women who stepped away from sewing machines or stepped onto soap boxes, uncertain of what they'd undertaken.

At work, my shoulders tensed when I saw editors huddled

together. I tried to read the body language of those we tallied in the "uncommitted" column. When I wasn't working, I was strategizing with Sol, coordinating with others on the committee, sitting in the dive bar a block from the newspaper looking for opportunities to talk to colleagues. I watched my back when I walked to my car after work or drove into my driveway.

On the day of the vote, soft murmurs filled the hallway as everyone who was not considered management filed into the room we called the "library," where reporters could look up stories in past issues of the newspaper and leave with decades-old ink smudging the sleeves of shirts and blouses. One representative of the union and one representative of management could challenge anyone who might not have a legitimate right to vote. Their votes would be set aside, only opened if the tally was close enough for them to make a difference. Then, individual determinations would be made about whether they were authorized to vote.

The union disputed the vote of the college journalism student who covered high school football games on Friday nights and hoped to be hired full-time. We challenged the editor emeritus, who was driven in from the nursing home where he listened to the police scanner—the way he had when he was the editor—and called the newsroom if he heard about a fire that he thought we might have missed.

The result was close, and the votes we challenged were thrown out by the local labor relations board. The newspaper appealed. Sol wasn't worried—the National Labor Relations Board never overruled the local, he explained.

But he had never organized a union where the publisher's son was a member of the United States Congress—at least, that was the only reason we could come up with for the NLRB reinstating the challenged ballots. The union needed to win by one vote. The final tally was a tie.

We lost, but the knowledge stayed in my body, a low purr like an electric typewriter waiting for my fingers to begin typing.

•

During the presidential election campaign of 2016, women who supported Hillary Clinton gathered in the virtual space of private Facebook groups like Pantsuit Nation. Stirred by an election in which one candidate was female and the other boasted of assaulting women he found attractive, women shared experiences of harassment, inequality, humiliation, dehumanization, and sexual assault with women they knew only over the internet but with whom they felt a sisterhood. Often they said they had never told anyone these stories—not even a partner. They listened to each other. They analyzed. They affirmed. They amplified each other's voices. They did what they did at Bryn Mawr and in circles formed by Belenky and her colleagues.

On January 21, 2017, they marched. Millions of women. In rural areas, in major cities, in nursing homes, across the country and the world. They marched. They sang. They nursed their babies, pushed their sons in strollers and their mothers in wheelchairs. They helped their daughters paint signs, held hands with their husbands, their mothers, their daughters, their lovers, their friends.

I was among them. I wanted my body counted. I wanted my body to count. I marched with younger women who had never marched before. Rain fell steadily as we stood on the grass along the river that runs through the heart of Portland, Oregon, too far away to hear the women speaking on stage, even with a sound system amplifying their voices. When we were finally able to march, wet and cold, we looked up and saw people gathered in red brick parking garages and windowed office buildings, waving and draping hand-lettered signs over ledges. Men and women. Little boys and little girls. On one street corner, a group of women singing a capella. On another, the rhythm of sticks on overturned buckets. Underneath it all, the soft humming of awakening hearts echoing off bridges and skyscrapers.

We marched for different reasons that day, all some version of bread or roses. Some for equal pay. Some for reproductive rights. Some for the love of another woman. Some to protest an election they believed had been marred by misogyny and a fear on the part of white men that they were losing their power. Some to claim dignity that the new president did not afford women, immigrants, Muslims. All of them using their bodies to find their voice, learning that the intellectual understanding of injustice shifts into a powerful force when bodies move together purposefully.

After, some analysts predicted the march would be a failure if it wasn't transformed into coordinated political action with clear legislative goals, identified leaders, strategies. That happened. In 2018, an unprecedented number of women ran for political office, with more women elected to the U.S. House of Representatives than ever before. Many more made phone calls, wrote letters, and showed up at town hall meetings.

I think of the women who walked out of the mills in Lowell and Lawrence and the silk factories of Paterson, New Jersey. I think of the women who jumped from the ninth floor of the Triangle Shirtwaist Factory, holding hands with each other for courage.

I think of Rosa Parks who sat her body down to speak up. No one had a plan for what would happen next. But for more than a year after, thousands of African Americans—many of the women employed as domestic workers—walked to their jobs in parts of Montgomery, Alabama, far from the neighborhoods where they lived, boycotting a segregated bus system, finding voice and solidarity as they put one foot in front of the other.

I think of my own failed effort to unionize the Muncie *Star* and how it didn't significantly change wages. But it changed me, helped me understand the power of a voice, helped me understand that leadership is not about title and position, but about body and voice, and that's what brings about change.

The Fires of Dismemberment

I wonder what I could do to make her hair weep, to fall to the ground, first a single strand, then another, until it was dropping in clumps gray and matted like dryer lint. I wonder what would make her skin peel back, curling like the white bark of birch branches in a campfire, hot and glowing, exposing soft wood. What would wake her from her sleep, perhaps her name called from the entry, the sound of soft soles on the oak stairs. I think how she would panic when she felt herself paralyzed, unable to make her legs swing from the bed to the floor or her arm reach for the phone, as she hears the click of the doorknob and recognizes, even though she is in silhouette in the doorway, the person she fired that morning.

She is frozen. She is burning. She is falling to the ground one body part after another. She is on her knees on the floor, scampering after the body parts as they roll under the chair, into the corner. One by one, she retrieves a liver, a thumb, a bit of toe, stuffs them into the cavity of her empty body, not sure where each belongs or how to attach it, desperate to be whole.

Revenge. From the Latin: *re:* "again" + *vindicare:* "assert a claim, claim as one's own; avenge, punish."

•

The summer before third grade, Sarah moved into the house behind ours, next to Chrissy, my best friend. Now I had two friends. They were even Catholic, so we would all go to school together. In September, Chrissy and Sarah were in Sister Agatha's class. I was in Mr. George's. Chrissy and Sarah sat together on the bus. Only two to a seat. They laughed about things I couldn't hear. Their class went to the cafeteria for lunch before ours. One day, when I went to sit with them, Sarah slid her green marbleized plastic tray over to the empty spot on the table next to her. "Saved," she said.

On the ride home, I imagined Sarah getting off the bus, me accidentally on purpose bumping her so that her books, covered in brown paper cut from grocery bags, scattered, and her bolting to retrieve them just as the bus lurched forward, the bus hitting her, rolling over her, cutting her in two, and Chrissy screaming, and me putting my arms around her, because I am her best friend.

Revenge. To claim as one's own.

•

"Restorative justice offers a new model of justice for victims and criminals alike. It builds on the notion that punishment does not provide an opportunity for the offender to feel forgiven or for the victim to forgive."

She takes a sip of water and scans the people scattered in too many rows of chairs in a Sunday School classroom in the basement of a church. She has handouts.

"Without forgiveness, the offender is frozen in a moment of violence, of evil. The victim is frozen in the experience that was wounding. Forgiveness, research shows, facilitates closure and healing for both, along with reconciliation to the community." Her voice drops with finality.

I want to get up from the dented metal folding chair I am

sitting in, walk down the center aisle as though answering an altar call, as though I've found Jesus, push my fingers into her sockets and rip out her eyes. Then turn and walk back down the aisle and toss the eyeballs on the table at the back of the room where they roll between the plastic trays of cookies.

Reconcile. From the Latin *reconcilare: re-* "again" + *concilare:* "make friendly."

•

I saw photographs of people at the finish line at the Boston Marathon, people without legs. I read how the pressure cooker used as a bomb threw shrapnel laterally, not blowing "up" but blowing "out," nails and ball bearings finding lower limbs. The smell of sulfur and burnt hair.

I read about a family, the father looking down and seeing his son, eight years old, not dead, but so close, and the father turning away from his dying son to save his daughter who was missing one of her legs. His wife would lose an eye. I wonder what a father sees in a still breathing child that instantly overcomes the denial, the instinct to try to save him, or just to stay. Even reports of trial testimony didn't say what the father saw. I wonder what part of a boy's body is the height of an adult knee. I wonder cavity. I wonder torso. I wonder burning, skin peeled back. When the boy's parents pleaded for the life of the man who planted the bombs, they said nothing about punishment or forgiveness, nothing about justice, nothing about "making friendly again." They just didn't want to tell their story at every death penalty appeal. They didn't want to have to revisit; they couldn't remember.

Remember. From the Latin *re-* "again" + *membrum:* "limb, member of the body, part." In English, "sense of person belonging to a group."

•

"It's a pressure cooker," he says about the place where we work, moments before she uses her cell phone to trigger the blow that sends sharp shards flying into the porous flesh of cubicle walls and the neck of a tender resume. We are no longer rolling with the punches. We are frozen in denial; we are burning with rage, falling, crawling around, peering under desks to see what might be retrieved, stuffed back into the body that is bleeding out. I am stunned. I am paralyzed. I cannot speak to say, "Stop, that is a healthy limb you are about to amputate."

The Synchronicity of Healing

Before dawn, the river is black, reflecting lights from downtown buildings at the water's edge. We hear a train whistle on the tracks that parallel the river, the occasional car rattle on the metal bridge that spans the divide. The earthy dampness smells like morning in a rain forest.

At this hour, the water is smooth, and we don't have to struggle to keep the boat set, stable. We tap the oar handles down at the end of the stroke to pop the blades out of the water, then roll the oars so that the blades are parallel with the surface. This feathering allows them to skim just above the water like the wings of a gull until we have floated as far forward as we can in our seats, arms reaching across bent knees, energy coiled in our bodies. We square the blades again and drop them into the water a split second before pushing against feet locked onto the boat. We feel the surge of power that propels the shell.

Then, we repeat. Repeat in a rhythm set by the port and starboard rowers closest to the stern. We each watch the shoulders of the woman in the seat in front to match the swing of her body at the end of the stroke, to feather the blade at precisely the same time, to start sliding the seat and stopping it exactly when she does, adjusting the speed of the movement in between to accommodate for shorter legs or longer torso. Focus. Only the coxswain speaks. The slightest disparity in the synchronous movement can tip the balance of this narrow, light shell. Readjusting requires coming into silent harmony with one another. We leave everything on the dock but this single-minded concentration on hands, arms, back, legs, feet, glutes, hamstrings, quads, pecs, lats. Core. Breath.

•

When we introduced ourselves on the first day of our learn-to-row class, we were asked what brought us to the river. Some had rowed in college. Some had family members who rowed. I'd happened across an announcement and been attracted to what sounded more fun than the circuit training I'd been doing at the gym to try to stem the muscle deterioration that seemed to be accelerating now that I am in my sixties. When Jo introduced herself, she pointed to me and said, "It was her idea."

Jo said yes without hesitation. Just as she said yes when I asked if she wanted to go to the 2015 Women's World Cup, try a new restaurant, come to a reading I was giving. Not that my ideas drive our friendship. I said yes to her accompanying me to an academic conference in Buenos Aires, to attending a performance of contemporary music, to using a fallen log to cross a river on the trail we were hiking. Outside of our friendship, Jo said yes to becoming a dean at the college where she taught. I said yes to going back to school at 52 for a PhD when I stumbled upon a program that looked interesting—not unlike the way I'd found rowing. Three years before we signed up to row, Jo said yes to a risky and agonizing treatment for kidney cancer that had metastasized to her lungs.

This notion of having to show up at the boathouse for 5 A.M. practice because our teammates depend on us to fill a seat in the boat is new to both of us. Aside from my freshman year of high school, when I played left wing on a field hockey team for a few months before my family moved and I enrolled in a school with no sports teams for girls, I have never played team sports. As an adult, I skied, played tennis, ran, and, at times, competed in triathlons. Jo, taller than I am and two years older, played basketball in high school under rules that prohibited her from crossing the center court line or dribbling too many times before passing. In the 1960s, such exertion was considered too much for fragile girl bodies needed for reproduction.

Our teammates in this novice boat chuckle when we tell them this. We are forty years older than some of them. Most grew up after Title IX created more opportunities for women in sports.

If I'd been paying attention, I would have recognized the signs of synchronicity, of both of us being summoned by the river to heal—me, newly and involuntarily retired after working for a toxic dean in higher education; Jo, whose simultaneous, but planned, retirement from a different university was punctuated by regular CT scans to look for any recurrence of the tumors in her lungs. I would have noticed it in the random way rowing crossed our paths, in our absence of questioning what it would entail, in our lack of hesitation in answering yes.

•

Almost fifteen years before, Sister Madonna Buder told me her story of synchronicity and healing, of being called, reading signs, saying yes. I interviewed her in her manufactured home in an over-55 community. I knew what everyone in the world of running and triathlon knew about her—her World Ironman records for women over sixty; victories and bike crashes, broken bones, resilience. Inevitable comparisons to "the flying nun." Grit. Perseverance. Courage.

She wore a gray velour track suit that day, Brooks running shoes, and a white turtleneck printed with red and green Christmas bells. A large gold crucifix hung on a chain in the center of her nearly flat chest. She had just run home from morning mass. Literally. While Sister warmed a glazed donut in the toaster oven and the smell of coffee permeated the air, I looked around: pictures and statues of Mary on end tables, the coffee table, shelves of an entertainment center, juxtaposed with gold-colored statues of winged victors—trophies from top finishes in marathons, triathlons, Ironmans. I contemplated the irony of this woman, expected to live a life of humility and prayer, becoming known for the extraordinary capabilities of her muscles, bones, capillaries, cartilage, even more noteworthy because of the age at which she started competing.

I sat across from her, my yellow legal tablet on the table, my journalist persona.

"Tell me why you became a nun."

She folded her hands on the table, like a good student. "Oh, you want to start there," she said, then told a story that came so easily it seemed she'd told it before—if not to reporters, to herself. A story of a woman who believed she was surrendering to vocation—the word means a "call or summons"—refusing to recognize doubt and signs of unsuitability. A story of stubbornness and defiance and isolation, of organizational bullying, and a story of healing that started when she took up running at the age of forty-eight.

•

I didn't know about Sister Madonna when I first raced her in the 1989 Coeur d'Alene Triathlon, fifteen years before our interview. It was my second race, and I'd entered it because Coeur d'Alene, a lakefront resort city in north Idaho, was close to where I lived. And though it was also close to Sister Madonna's home in Spokane, Washington, she was there because the race attracted the top names on the triathlon circuit. She had already made a name for herself in three Hawaii Ironmans, one of the most challenging athletic competitions in the world—a 2.4 mile swim followed by a 112 mile bike, finishing with a 26.2 mile run, equal to a marathon.

The Coeur d'Alene Triathlon was the shorter Olympic distance for triathlons. It began with a swim of 1.5 kilometers. I wore a sleeveless wetsuit. My age was inked in indelible black marker on my left deltoid and left calf.

Just before the gun echoed across the water to start the race, I waded into the lake from a narrow strip of beach, my breath catching at the cold. Water leaked into my wetsuit forming a thin layer that was heated by my body. I peed one last time, the warmth spreading down my legs under the neoprene. When the race started, I hopped along the bottom of the lake until I found a depth for swimming and became part of a mass of flailing arms and legs. I was one of the last out of the water, and when I look now at the splits for the race, I see that as I tottered up the beach on feet so numb they felt like stubs, Sister Madonna had a five minute lead on her bike.

Swinging a leg over my bike, I headed for the 40 kilometer bike course. I barely noticed the marsh where buffleheads and mallards glided, the red barn, the smell of wheat fields ready for harvest or the yellow pine trees that lined the climb to the crest of the final hill. I was a stronger cyclist than swimmer. Each time I passed a competitor, I looked at the age marked on her shoulder.

I did not pass any nuns.

Sister Madonna had a twenty-minute lead on me by the time I racked my bike, dropped my helmet, and set off on the 10 kilometer run. Only a world record holder could have caught her then. I crossed the finish line ninth out of the twelve women in my 36-40 age group. Sister Madonna had picked up another six-and-a-half minutes on me during the run.

When the complete race results arrived in the mail I looked closely at the times for women in the older age groups. That's when I saw Sister Madonna Buder's name and time and age: fifty-nine. That's when I started to wonder about her story. I wondered, too, about the women I saw on the course whose arms displayed ages over forty. I knew that like me, they'd had limited opportunities to enjoy sports, discover athletic ability. I wondered what their stories were. What called them? How did they find their stride? Had they braved the kind of taunts and ostracism that "tomboys" suffered? Did they find a community of women who understood, even mentored them?

•

At the boathouse, the more experienced rowers greet those of us learning to row with smiles and enthusiasm. They wear T-shirts and visors with the club name. They are tall and short, wiry and robust. They ask our names and remember them when they see us again. They encourage us to join the club after the class ends. "You'll see," one says, "you'll get addicted to this."

I wonder how welcoming they would be if they were in the boat with me. Five weeks into the class, I mistakenly put a port oar into my starboard oarlock. I struggle to remember everything I need to do—how to hold the oars, to keep my posture upright, to notice if the boat is listing to one side, to remember my seat number so that when the coxswain shouts to me to join in or drop out, I respond without hesitation. The safety of the boat could depend on it. I catch a crab—the blade of the oar is caught by competing forces in the water and the handle slams into my chest with a drive that threatens to send me overboard. The boat has to stop while I regain control. I am embarrassed, despite assurances that this happens to everyone. I don't want to be the weak link.

Nonetheless, before the class ends, I ask Jo, "Do you want to join the club?"

"Yes."

Practice is scheduled so we can be on the water while it is calm and rowers can make it to work on time, so even though Jo and I have both just retired, we set our alarms for 4:15 A.M. Rowing becomes a routine, a practice, a meditation. The coach rides in a motorized launch, runs us through drills, corrects body position. There is more to learn. Subtle moves, like contracting the leg on the high side of the boat, or moving the oar handles a centimeter up or down, can help bring the shell into balance. There is no room for thoughts other than those needed to move the boat smoothly, efficiently, together.

We don't talk in the boat or as we get the boat ready or put it away. No one asks what anyone does outside the boathouse; all that matters is what we do when we are together. The boat digs into the soft flesh of my shoulder when I carry it, but no one suggests that Jo and I might need help because we are older. They do not expect us to compensate for lack of power with wisdom or humor. They do not treat us like we're cute because we are learning this at our age. We accept each other's quirks and mistakes, strengths and limitations, because we are a boat, a community—not individuals.

Jo doesn't tell anyone in the boathouse about her cancer. When she was first diagnosed—when her kidney was removed and she was told there was no sign the cancer had progressed to other organs or lymph nodes and there was no need for chemotherapy or radiation—she told family, friends, colleagues. Almost two years later, a CT showed tumors in her lungs, shadows the size of sesame seeds. She was hospitalized for a week at a time over the course of several months as toxins were pumped into her body in an attempt to convince her immune system that it had to rally, had to step up to this challenge. Jo's assistant set up a schedule so there was someone at her bedside round-the-clock, another set of eyes and ears to watch for signs of a sudden drop in her blood pressure or notice that she was talking nonsense, seeing sheep dance on her bed sheets. And so she never felt alone. Her pale skin became flushed and hot, pink and itchy like she was covered in poison ivy. We rubbed lotion on her legs and arms and back in an effort to soothe, slept in a leather recliner in a semi-lit room that smelled like antiseptic and Neutrogena.

I wrote notes almost daily on an internet site where people who cared about Jo could keep up on her progress and send her messages that often framed cancer as a competition, a race she could win, an opponent she could defeat. "You're strong," they said, as though cancer defeats only the weak.

When the treatment was over, the progress of the tumors stemmed, the meal trains discontinued, the word "remission" said in the same sentence as her name, Jo and I talked about how cancer defines someone. Becomes part of your identity. Marks you. How you always *have cancer* or are a *cancer survivor*. We talked about whether people avoided her or avoided asking about her health and whether others thought about her only in terms of her health. How does one find the balance? We talked about how she could come into harmony with diagnosis and treatment and a new normal, how she could incorporate her doctor's prognosis at the end of the immunotherapy—"think years, not decades"—into decisions about everything from home improvements to international travel. She asked a counselor, "When do you tell someone you've just started dating about a cancer that might come back?" The counselor deflected the question—"Everyone in your age group has or will have health issues." Was that approach avoidance or the new normal?

Jo tells me she isn't trying to hide her cancer from her teammates, but she doesn't mention it because three years after immunotherapy, she isn't sure it's relevant. We talk one day about how this means no one on the rowing team thinks of her in terms of cancer. What does she gain by being with people who assume she is as healthy as she looks? What is the cost of withholding from people something both profoundly meaningful and temporally insignificant? How much has cancer become part of her identity? How vulnerable do we have to be to be part of a community?

•

In 1959, when Dorothy Marie Buder took her vows as a Sister of the Good Shepherd, a nun left her family and lived with members of her order, drawing strength from that community rather than from a husband. She wore a long white gown to signify that she became the "bride of Christ," was given a new name, a symbol of her new identity.

After Vatican II, when nuns began wearing modified habits and then common dress, many took back the names they were given at birth. Those of us who were in Catholic schools returned from summer vacation to find Sister Mary Joseph had become Sister Nancy O'Leary and Sister Incarnation was now Sister Catherine Pucci.

Sister Madonna kept her name, even though she added her family name, Buder.

Madonna is from the Italian "my lady." It became associated with Mary through glorified artistic representations: *The Madonna in Majesty* by Cimabue, *Madonna of the Carnation* by Leonardo da Vinci, the Madonna with Child, with Saints, Angels, Flowers, Birds. Paintings by Botticelli, Fra Angelico, van Eyck, Michelangelo. *A Gentleman in Adoration before the Madonna* by Moroni. It is not a humble name. Sister told me that she didn't request it, and I don't ask her why she kept it. She tells me how being given that name—and the synchronicity of her grandfather's deathbed conversion and the propitious day chosen for her to take her vows—was evidence of having been called, proof of specialness that countered her superiors' doubts about whether she was right for the convent. Doubts that remained years after she took her vows.

Sister Madonna had not been at her first assignment for long before she became the subject of a community meeting that she still refers to as a "kangaroo court." The other sisters stood one at a time and gave examples of Sister Madonna's failings as a person and as a member of the community—vague references to a lack of humility and cooperation.

Sister Madonna was stoic; she denied the Mother Superior's report that she found Sister Madonna in the chapel afterward in tears. She told me, "They didn't win that day," that her request for a transfer wasn't a sign of defeat or weakness.

•

At the time, it didn't occur to me that whatever compelled me to explore Sister Madonna's story might have been a sign, might have relevance for me down the road. I thought my interest in her was as one triathlete to another, one female body to another, two women discouraged by culture and convention from pursuing athletic interests. Later I would read Carolyn Myss's book, *Sacred Contracts*, which draws on Jungian psychoanalytic theory to suggest that we are destined even before birth to encounter certain individuals in our lives at certain times. Some appear only briefly, some stay with us a long time, but each is there with a purpose, a message.

Someone on the rowing team asks Jo how long she and I have been friends. Jo smiles. "Since July 1, 1976." A different rower asks me how we met. "My husband and her ex-husband were family medicine residents together. We were the first group of residents' wives who planned to have careers even after our husbands set up practice. We bonded over that." Jo nods and recites the medical auxiliary pledge we were given to read, how it mandated that we keep the home hearth swept free of pettiness. She rolls her eyes the way I remember her doing that day in 1976. I recall that wives in the classes ahead of ours assured us that we'd get pregnant soon, reminded us that we wouldn't have to work because our husbands now had salaries. We forged friendships because we were breaking new ground, without mentors to guide us, and needed each other for support.

When our husbands finished, the class dispersed as we chose where to settle, build practices, raise children. Jo and I saw each other from time to time, but mostly we lost touch until she, newly divorced, moved to Portland, Oregon, and a few years later, as part of rebuilding our marriage, my husband and I also moved to Portland. Jo and I picked up our friendship the way we do with just a few people in our lives, the ones who have been with us at the turning points. The ease with which we reconnected was like riding a bike after a long absence.

Sacred contract.

•

When Sister Madonna finished telling me about the accusations from her community, she dropped her chin, looked at her empty coffee mug, her confident voice softer. She shook her head almost imperceptibly. "I must not have been that close to the other nuns or I would have picked up on the signs that I wasn't fitting in." I wanted to reach across the table, touch her hand gripping the mug. To this point, her story had been practiced, told with the confidence of an athlete. This admission seemed fresh, raw.

Her chin lifted again, and her voice shifted as she regained her footing. She related how she finished graduate degrees, then spent eight months in San Francisco, four months in North Dakota, time in New York. In each new assignment, more criticism. Some said she was too innovative; some said she was too conservative.

By the time Sister Madonna arrived in Spokane in 1971, her frequent moves marked her as a misfit. She had difficulty explaining the tension that dogged her wherever she went. She shrugged her shoulders as she told me her sisters said she was "lacking in community," a loner. Obedient but unpredictable.

The Spokane nuns soon had grievances too. There was another tribunal.

I ask Sister Madonna why she stayed, why she never asked to be released from her vows as so many nuns did. She told me she didn't want to be driven out. That would have been a defeat.

She acknowledged the toll it took. "My spirit was dying," she said. She went to a spiritual retreat on the Oregon coast. A priest there recommended she run on the beach.

I told her I started running on the Oregon coast too. The sand is firm at low tide, the rhythm of waves like a mantra, repeating. The ocean a reminder of the feminine, of power.

When she returned from the coast, she continued to work long hours, felt isolated from her community. She burned out. Her community released her from all her duties.

Spokane is a city near mountains and lakes, bisected by a river that flows into the Columbia, the smell of lilac and cedar. Bored, hurting, Sister Madonna remembered how she felt running at the coast, and she ran—down Indian Trail Road, on the path beside the river, up trails on the nearby mountain. Legs burning. Lungs aching. She felt her problems diminished by the magnitude of the sky and the mountain and a river that didn't see boulders as an obstacle.

She began to race. The very qualities that had been a source of conflict for her in the convent now served her as an athlete.

Grit. Perseverance. Courage.

Power.

Purpose.

All the stories I'd read about Sister Madonna portrayed only the heroic narrative, the synchronicity of her being advised by a priest to take up running and how that released a desire and a gift, replaced one identity with another, one community with another. I didn't know why she shared the more vulnerable story with me, and I was unsure what to believe about it. I could believe she chafed against her vow of humility, believe her community found her aloof and arrogant. Who would be more difficult to live with in a community of nuns committed to poverty and humility than someone who believed in her own exceptionalness? I can also believe in the cruelty of nuns who confuse humility with mediocrity. Sister Madonna's depiction of her public disgrace is reminiscent of those times in Catholic school when a nun publicly shamed a child who had transgressed, those times when a nun shamed me.

•

When the new dean summoned me to a disciplinary hearing just a few months after she was hired, I had to think back to high school, to being summoned to the convent, to remember the last time I'd been reprimanded. The accusations were preposterous and untrue and difficult to refute because they were impossible to prove.

I was not stoic. My heart beat rapidly. My hands shook. I babbled defensively. My colleagues would have been supportive, but the dean told me I would be fired if I told them I'd been disciplined.

More bullying followed. Gaslighting, in which the dean held me accountable to rules that changed without warning. She undermined me with students, marginalized me, demoted me. I knew she wanted me to resign before my contract ended.

I ranted to my husband with each new incident. The injustice. The exhaustion of trying to make sense of the senseless. The feeling of isolation from a community that had embraced me. Almost as frequently, I talked to Jo. As a friend, her compassion buoyed me. As a dean whose academic career was much longer than mine, her perspective that I was being treated unfairly sustained me. "I don't want to quit." I said to both her and my husband. "I don't want her to win."

But bullying is dependent on a power imbalance; it's not a fair fight, not something that can be overcome with grit or perseverance.

When, after two years, my contract was not renewed and I was effectively fired, I expected to feel the way I did at the end of a triathlon—bent over with pain and exhaustion, but finally, able to breathe deeply. I expected to feel a sense of accomplishment that I hadn't surrendered.

Instead, I was angry. I engaged in fantasies of vengeance and retaliation. I was bored. The days seemed endless. I noticed dusty floors and dirty countertops and resented that I had time to attend to them. I had interests: I wrote. I exercised. I volunteered. It all felt like killing time, waiting for something with meaning to emerge. I applied for jobs, but I knew that being in my mid-sixties, I should not expect to be competitive, especially in academia, especially without a letter of reference from my previous employer. Still, I was hurt when I was passed over. I was jealous of the way Jo retired. Our post-retirement lives looked the same, but I envied the way she got to control the end of her career, the way her achievements were properly noted, celebrated, and archived. The darkness of the wet Northwest winter seeped into my bones where I also stored my anger.

•

When I first start to row, I don't notice the weight of my resentment dissipating on the river like early morning fog. On the water, I empty my mind to focus on the motions of my body as I move through the sequence: push down with my heels just after my blade connects with the water, hang on the oar handle—wait until my seat is pushed back completely before I swing my back in unison with the seven other women in the boat, then, at the last moment, pull the oar into my body, keeping my core engaged.

My quads start to bulge the way they did when I trained for triathlons. I feel my biceps strain against the sleeves of my sweat-soaked shirt, feel exhilarated at the end of ten hard pushes—a "power ten"—at a stroke rate greater than our usual pace, notice bleeding blisters on the palms of my hands only when practice is over.

I pull my own weight.

The effort of hoisting the boat overhead and resting it on my shoulders starts to feel easier. I think it is due to new muscle; I don't realize there is more lightness in every move I make.

Some mornings, just as we are heading back to the dock after a hard row, I notice the office buildings shining in first light. I look up and see clouds overhead starting to show pink. I hear the city waking up, meeting another day, alive. I think that whatever happens the rest of the day, I have had this time on the river, in the company of women.

The rhythm of rowing settles into my muscles. I bring it home with me. The need to stay in the moment. The importance of balance. The feeling of my own power moving through me.

At the end of the summer, Jo and I sign up for our first race—5,000 meters on a lake near Seattle. We schedule extra practices with the other novices who will be in the boat. We work harder, longer, better.

A few weeks before the race, Jo gets her regular CT. In the three years since she completed immunotherapy, these have become almost routine. She texts me: Her lung nodules show growth. There is a new tumor, very small, in her spine.

"Can I come over?"

"Yes."

She comes over and we do what friends do when there is bad news.

Jo is prescribed an oral medication with side effects that include high blood pressure, fatigue, diarrhea, sores on the hands and feet. "I don't know if I will be able to race," Jo says, "and I don't want to let the boat down."

The race is canceled due to exceptionally high winds.

Synchronicity.

We are nearing the end of our first season of rowing. Jo texts me: Headache. Dizzy. BP 180. Not rowing today. With high blood pressure, the exertion of rowing could cause a stroke. Jo tells the coach she is being treated for cancer. The coach seats Jo in front of me in the boat. Stroke partners. The irony of that label is not lost on us. Her shoulders are covered by a UPF shirt because the drugs make her pale skin even more sun sensitive. I watch them to know when to swing my body. I watch them to see if they start to slump, if she looks fatigued. I listen to her breathe. We are not to talk in the boat, but I whisper: "Are you OK?" When I sense she is tired, I will the coxswain to rotate us out, give us a rest.

Over the winter, we continue to get up in the dark, drive to the boathouse to row on machines, be with our community. The boathouse smells like sweat and grease. We listen to playlists from the 80s, rhythmic tunes that recall jazzercise classes, keep us engaged. Without the need to balance the boat or feather the oar or move in concert with seven other women,

I can concentrate on the movement of my body, build muscle and muscle memory. There is opportunity to talk, to pass the time, to ask about lives outside the boat. To get to know each other at a different level. Some of the more experienced rowers are in their sixties. Unlike Jo and me, they have been rowing for decades. Even without Title IX, they found their way to a sport where they could harness the power of their bodies, compete, be with other women.

Jo has a CT every three months. The first shows the tumors shrinking 40 percent, the next one, a little more.

By the time we are back on the water the following spring, the river is high and fast and muddy. The coxswain steers us past logs that have washed into the water with the spring thaw. I am surprised at my longing to be in the boat, even on days when it is raining and the water is rough. "A bad day on the river is better than a good day on a rowing machine," I tell my husband as I roll out of bed in the dark. Each day the sun lights up the sky a bit earlier. We pass a sea lion resting on the abutment of a bridge, hear the cry of an osprey overhead.

Over the winter, Jo's oncologist added medications to lower blood pressure, stop diarrhea. Jo found that a vitamin cocktail dripped into her veins boosted her energy. The side effects of Jo's treatment are more manageable, or perhaps have just become the new normal.

Her CT is stable.

Stable.

Stable.

Stable.

I notice that when Jo and I are out of the rowing rotation for a brief rest, she sits up tall, breathes with more ease than the previous autumn. While there are still days when she has trouble lifting the boat out of the water, carrying it back to the boathouse, she notices she can't fit into last summer's T-shirt. "My arms are too big," she says, smiling.

"Should we join a group rowing on Lago Maggiore, between Italy and Switzerland?"

"Yes."

"Should we go to every Women's World Cup venue in France in 2019 and guest row with a club in every city we visit?"

"Yes."

"What would we talk about if we didn't have rowing?" Jo asks me one day.

I wonder if we would talk more about cancer, about health. We don't take long walks or hike any more because the soles of her feet are sore, though not a problem pushing in the boat. I wonder if we would respond to her fatigue with more lunch dates and phone banking for political candidates. I wonder if we would contemplate traveling to Italy, France. I wonder what that new normal would have been.

We sign up to race in the Row for the Cure regatta.

This is not our first race. In that race, I could barely keep up with the pace set by younger and stronger rowers in the front of the boat combined with the tendency of inexperienced novices to explode at the start. The splash of flailing oars drenched my handle, and I struggled to hold onto it. I missed a lot of water. I didn't feel I showed what I could do, the results of my hard training. And yet, it was also clear that even at my best there was an insurmountable gap between my ability and those of both the younger rowers and the sixty-year-olds who have been rowing for decades.

I was no Sister Madonna.

Jo's experience was similar, perhaps more difficult to bear because while our boat had a handicap for age, there is no handicap for rowers being treated for cancer. She brushed away tears after our first race. "I feel like I am the weak link," she said to the coach. The coach put her arms around Jo. "You bring other strengths to the boat." I think:

Grit.

Perseverance.

Courage.

The day we are to Row for the Cure, the lake is flat, the lanes for the 1,000 meter course visible from the team tent where it is shady and a table is stacked with fruit and cookies and deli platters. The sky is cloudless, the wind light. Before the race, the novice team gathers in a circle on dry grass that pricks the backs of our bare legs. We are wearing matching blue shirts and visors with the team name and logo. We talk about the people in our lives we are dedicating the race to: *Mother. Sister. Partner. Friend.* Some living. Some not. Jo takes a deep breath and tells the team she is rowing for herself. She tells them why. When she is unable to say more, she turns to me.

"I could tell you," I say, "what Jo has been rowing through—what cancer and cancer treatment does to rowing—the fatigue, high blood pressure. . . "

"And diarrhea," Jo says, interrupting.

"I wasn't going to mention that."

The women laugh, relieved to have the mood lightened. I reach over to Jo, sitting beside me on the grass. I take her hand. Her skin is warm. I go on:

"But I want to tell you what rowing does to a body with cancer. Jo is stronger than she was a year ago. Her body is responding to the training despite the drugs that make her tired. And everyone in the boat contributes to that."

We don't row for a cure; rowing doesn't cure cancer. It doesn't even beat cancer. I understand the value of positive thinking, but the expectation that grit and perseverance and courage can defeat cancer only adds guilt to the load the cancer patient is carrying. But progress in rowing—that's something achievable, that's a goal to focus on, a competition where grit and perseverance have a role. Rowing may not change Jo's health, but it changes her body and changes how she feels and how she feels in her body.

Rowing doesn't heal the wounds left by a bully any more than it cures cancer. But during my time on the river—like time spent running on a path winding through the woods—I am aware of my own power in my body. I feel exhausted not from being in a toxic work environment but from pushing through a physical barrier. I breathe in the morning air as the sun starts to reflect on the black water. It lifts me up the way eight women lift a sixty-two-foot boat and settle it on their shoulders.

HOME

The Grammar of Untold Stories

My grandmother spoke little English. Her teeth were yellow and chipped. She smelled like a book that hadn't been opened in a long time. When she hugged, she pulled me into her soft body forever, repeating my name in a way I didn't recognize. My face pressed into her bosom; I stiffened at the mustiness of her dark dress. When she released me, I could breathe again. I'd done my duty.

•

When I fell in love with my husband I fell in love with his grandmother and with their love as thick and rich as the tomato sauce she served at every family gathering. As a boy, my husband spent Saturdays with her, and together they tore advertising circulars and old magazines into bits, tossed the colorful paper fragments into the air like confetti, and then vacuumed them up. I sucked his stories into my narrative, using his family like caulk to fill in the empty spaces where the wind whistled through mine. When his grandmother, as short and round as my own, pulled me into her softness, I didn't want to leave.

•

It was my husband's idea. We were going to Budapest for a vacation.

"As long as we're there, we could visit your grandmother's village," he said. "Do a little research. You might find a family member who still lives there."

With no one alive who could tell me, I had to do "a little research" to even learn the name of the village where my grandmother was born. I found it online, on her 1925 petition for US citizenship. The copy I printed reproduced the smudges and irregularities of the microfiche document along with names and dates and places. My grandmother's history was strewn on the page like agates on the beach—precious stones unearthed by rough sea, waiting to be gathered. Her village, just a short ride from Budapest by train.

•

My father, her youngest, was born in the United States. Though bilingual, he didn't teach me any Hungarian, except *fing a fürdőkádban*, a phrase that he said meant "a fart in the bathtub," meaning "unwelcome, out of place, disturbing the surface smoothness." Maybe even immigrant. Our family name, Ruskai, was less obviously Hungarian than Kovács, Tóth, or my grandmother's name, Nagy. People often asked me, "What are you?" My father told me it was none of their business. I was to answer: "American." He himself would make what he thought was a joke. "Hawaiian," he'd say, at a time when that, too, meant "not American." When the person inquiring stared back at him, trying to find a Pacific Islander in my father's angular features and olive skin, my father would deliver the punch line: "You know, Ruskai. Like Molokai." Then he'd chuckle. Even as a child, I knew it wasn't funny. I didn't understand until much later that he was deflecting his own embarrassment onto the person who seemed to question whether my father and his family belonged here. I think now of the irony in his choosing the name of an island where lepers were sent.

•

Ruskai. We pronounced it "Russ ki," rhyming with "eye." But in Hungarian, the *s* is pronounced "sz," and *kai* is pronounced "karee." We should have said "Rusz karee."

•

I called her Gramma Ruskai. She came to live with us when I was nine years old. By then, she no longer knew my name. She was unable to connect the fractured remnants of people and places that dusted her memory. She believed she was in Hungary and that the children who had died were still alive. When she called to them and they didn't answer, she got angry. I awoke one night to see her standing in the doorway of my bedroom, her thin cotton nightgown taut over her protruding abdomen. For a moment I mistook her silhouette for that of my pregnant mother. Then my grandmother spoke something I didn't understand, and I wondered how long she had been watching me. Some days my grandmother ran off, surprisingly quick for someone almost eighty. My mother would have to call my father to find her and coax her home in Hungarian, although nothing about where my grandmother lived said "home" to her.

Before she came to live with us, my grandmother lived in a house my grandfather built himself on the street behind the school where I went to kindergarten. I never went to her house after school. I never spent Saturdays cutting up pieces of colored paper. I don't remember going to her house for holidays or Sunday dinners—I had other grandparents for that. But in the few years after my grandfather died and before dementia left my grandmother living in her long term memories, I went with my father when he tilled the soil and sprinkled seeds for her garden, when the kitchen sink leaked, and once, when her basement flooded and left sediment on the cellar walls. I went because I liked being with my father without my sisters around. I don't remember having a conversation with my grandmother, and I didn't understand anything she and my father said to each other.

•

My knowledge of Hungary was scattered. I knew a little about St. Elizabeth, Queen of Hungary, from my book of Catholic saints, although the child's version of her story was abridged, missing details I learned about later—her abuse by her spiritual advisor, to whom she vowed obedience after the death of her husband. I knew bits about the 1956 Revolution from history books during the Cold War, but not the particulars of Soviet oppression. To prepare for the trip to Hungary that my husband and I were taking, I bought a Lonely Planet guidebook, a thick book of Hungarian history starting with migrations in 400 B.C., and two Hungarian novels regarded worthy enough to be translated into English.

•

My grandmother was born Erszébet Nagy. She died Elizabeth Ruskai. As a child, I fantasized that I was descended from a queen who was also a saint. Even then, I used my imagination to fill in the empty spaces where there should have been stories. I Googled my grandmother's birth name together with the village name—Hernadnémeti. I don't know what I thought I'd find. I'd already looked at the records available online and found only the passenger manifest for the ship she'd arrived on at Ellis Island. I did find a death notice for an Elizabeth Nagy in Wisconsin who had died just a month before. The obituary told how she had fled Hernadnémeti after the 1956 revolution. She was nine months pregnant. She made it to Ireland, then went into labor shortly after her plane took off from Dublin. The pilot aborted the trip, turned the plane around. Her son was born in the airport. A daring and courageous escape from Communist reprisals. I realized I knew more about this family's immigration story from a single newspaper clipping than I did my own. I found the son on Facebook. "Ask him for his recipe for liver dumpling soup," my husband said. The dish was a favorite of my father's, and my mother learned to make it the way my grandmother did. "If it's the same as yours," my husband said, "you'll know you're related."

•

Nagy, my grandmother's family name, is as common in Hungary as Jones or Smith is in the United States. It is pronounced "Noodg."

My father's name was Michael. In Hungarian, Mihály. Pronounced "Me high."

•

My grandmother died of a heart attack in the locked ward of a nursing home where my father placed her after my mother said she couldn't take care of both a senile old woman and a newborn. I haven't visited my grandmother's grave since the day she was buried, on my eleventh birthday. Her stories are deposited there, too, decomposing with her. I never asked my father about her, where she was born, what she was like. I don't know if he was embarrassed by her teeth or her difficulty speaking English. I don't know if he brought friends home after school. He died when I was nineteen and newly in love, when I believed the only stories that mattered were the ones my beloved and I would write.

Years after my father died, I was at a conference where one of the speakers was named "Mihály." When he was introduced, I heard my grandmother calling my father. I found myself standing in a queue at the speaker's table after the session, like a bead in a rosary. He was answering questions as he packed his briefcase. When it was my turn, I said, "My father's name was Mihály. I haven't heard that name in a long time." Then I felt my face redden, and I considered that I was being unprofessional, exposing a longing.

•

By the time my husband and I boarded our flight to Budapest, I'd read only as far as the Crusades in the history book. I was more interested in the guidebook and the novels.

Lonely Planet said Budapest's Keleti pályaudvar, which translates to "eastern train station," was the most modern and artistic railway station in Europe when it was built in the early 1880s, coinciding with the time my grandmother was born. The station's style is a mix of influences that reflect the country's conquests by Turks and Europeans. The platform smelled like pastry and diesel and warm bodies. I stepped outside. It was early morning and the light was good. I pulled my camera out of my backpack and looked through the viewfinder at the sun angled on windows with leaded panes. The need to negotiate lenses and f-stops felt overwhelming after a long flight and the effort to communicate about lost luggage. I reminded myself of lost opportunities. *Take the picture,* I told myself. But I didn't know how to take the photo that was not a tourist snapshot, the photo that said how I felt standing on the platform listening to people arriving and leaving, hearing words that meant nothing but were wrapped in the sounds and inflections of my father talking with my grandmother, sounds I hadn't heard in more than fifty years but made me feel held. I put the camera away and went back inside, took a paper slip with a number, and waited for that number to appear above one of the ticket windows. When it was my turn I bought two tickets to Miskolc, the closest stop to my grandmother's village. *Köszönöm.* "Thank you." The language guide says it's pronounced "kur-sur-nurm."

126

•

Nem beszélek magyarul.

I pronounced it like this: "I don't speak Hungarian."

You either speak Hungarian or you don't. It is an obscure and difficult language. You can't fake your way through lunch with your grandmother or an encounter with a Budapest ticket agent the way you can get by in Mexico with a couple of years of high school Spanish. Despite the DNA in my cells, my mouth did not know how to shape the syllables. To my husband, not only the words but the rhythm of them one after the other sounded alien. For me, the cadence of the language was specific to one time and place, to my grandmother talking to my father. I once heard Rilke read in the original German. I wasn't familiar enough with his work to know the poem. I heard the meaning not in the individual words and lines, but in the sounds that held feeling, the way a very young child might know emotion in a grandparent's murmurs before she knew that sounds formed words.

•

Hungary is a volcanic land with thermal baths flowing with healing water, and the cave baths near Miskolc are among the most visited outside Budapest. My husband and I walked to them from our bed and breakfast. Plump women in two-piece bathing suits and men with lean, sharp features like my father's stood under water streaming from the mouths of cement lions or walked on mosaic tiles through the rocky passages. I expected the smell of sulfur, like eggs boiled too long that explode on the stove, splattering bits of sticky albumen onto walls and windows, but the water smelled clean. Some pools were shallow, the water tepid. We negotiated the labyrinth until we entered the deepest reaches of the cave—a darkened room where the water was warmest and no one spoke. I closed my eyes and floated. I imagined this is what it felt like in the womb.

•

The drive from the cave baths to Hernadnémeti took only twenty minutes. The village wasn't mentioned in the guidebook, although the nearby Tokaj wine district was. We passed planted fields with hawks circling above. A few turns off the main road and we were there. Children and men and even older women with soft bodies rode one-speed bicycles on the narrow streets. The houses were cream-colored and mostly one-story with stucco walls and red clay roofs. White storks nested in chimneys. I looked at them through my binoculars, twisting the lens to bring the birds into focus. I could see how, nesting like that, the myth was born that storks bring babies, dropping them down the chimney like a gift from Saint Nicholas, hiding the truth about sex.

•

This is the story of how Hungary came to be: *Emese, a princess, was married to King Ügyek. She could not conceive. She was impregnated by a turul, and the dream she had of a mighty river flowing from her body foretold a descendant who would be the founder of Hungary.*

•

This is the story I heard growing up: My grandmother wanted to become a nun. When she was fifteen, her family forced her to marry an older man from a nearby village who was considered a "good catch." He came to America, where he worked as a gardener until he made enough money to send for her and their three children. I think my mother told me that story.

•

It was early in the day, but already too hot for us to be wandering among the uneven rows of granite and limestone

128

in Hernadnémeti's cemetery. Here and there, a tree provided a little shade. I was still wearing the T-shirt I'd worn on the plane, now dampening with sweat. Some graves had simple markers, some had obelisks, angels, carved wreaths. Kovács, Takács, Szabó, Kiss. There were tombs for entire families. Because my grandfather was from another village, I knew none would be marked Ruskai. There were too many engraved with Nagy to know if I should stop and pay my respects to this one or that one. Near the back of the cemetery, half obscured by weeds, were discarded tombstones, stacked against rocks like LPs in a vintage record store. Grave markers removed because no one paid the annual fees. Ancestors unhonored.

•

The first Hungarian novel I read took place in Italy with characters on their honeymoon. But in Magda Szabó's novel, *The Door*, I met Emerence, a woman whose past is a mystery, who prefers to be misunderstood than to reveal her story. She works as a maid and takes care of the people on her street, her cats, her employer's dog, and refugees from the violence of the secret police of the Nazi and later the Soviet occupiers. All she wants is to save enough money to build a tomb where she can be buried and into which she can move the bones of relatives who have passed.

•

Bryan Cartledge begins his history of Hungary, *The Will to Survive*, like this: "Nations need myths. Hungary, a country that became conscious of nationhood rather late in its history, has its fair share. Hungarian myths are more concerned with origins than with gods or heroes."

Even today, when you can swab the inside of your cheek and send it to *National Geographic* to get a map of your heritage, uncertainty surrounds the answer to the question of how Hungarians, with a language incomprehensible to their neighbors, came to be a cultural island in the center of Europe. Cartledge says the most likely explanation is that they migrated from western Siberia as part of a group of Finno-Ugrians, which splintered into smaller groups, one of which became the linguistic offshoot known as Magyars. Their identity is entwined with a language unique to them. Their language is how they know who they are. It is how they know that someone is a member of their tribe.

Magyar. It's pronounced like this: "Mudg yar." The language is softer than it looks on paper.

•

My grandmother's petition for citizenship, the sworn statement of her birth, her marriage, her children, and her immigration, had information new to me. I pulled the facts into this account: She was seventeen and my grandfather twenty-four when they married on February 10, 1899. My grandfather left for America a year later. One year and one month after he arrived in America, my grandmother gave birth to her first child, a son. She bore another son two years later, and a third two years after that. When the youngest was two, she and her three sons boarded the *Slavonia*, which arrived at Ellis Island on July 11, 1907. The petition does not list the daughter that I know was born in America, the one who died when she was nine years old. It does list my father's birth, in 1919, a year after the daughter died. My father, the replacement child, the fourth son, but the one who carried his father's name, Mihály.

My father ran away from home when he was fourteen. He went to a seminary to become a priest. My grandmother went after him, brought him back. That part of the story always surprised me, since I'd been told my grandmother herself wanted a religious life. Years later, my father and my mother met when they both joined the Third Order of St. Francis, the lay branch of the Franciscans, whose patron saint is Queen

Elizabeth of Hungary. My parents were both devout Catholics. My grandmother threatened not to come to their wedding. She told my maternal grandparents that their daughter would be unfaithful. I never understood why she would make that assumption.

The Catholic Church where my grandparents were married was easy to find; its steeple rose above the one-story houses in Hernadnémeti. I could hear the priest talking in the rectory when I knocked at the door, but he didn't answer. The curtains on the windows were closed. I wanted to find my grandparents' marriage record, to hold in my hands the original paper with my grandmother's signature and my grandfather's mark. Although I knew marriage records were kept in civic offices, not the church, I thought a priest might speak English.

My genealogy search had not led me to any family members. The man on Facebook, whose mother's name matched my grandmother's, called me "cousin" when he accepted my friend request, but I didn't have enough information for us to know if we really were related. He only knew one person in the village who spoke English, and she was out of the country.

My husband and I drove the narrow village roads searching for anything that looked like civic offices. We couldn't read the signs. We stopped at what looked like public buildings, first a school and then at what we discovered was a senior center, and asked if anyone spoke English. *Szia.* "See ah." It means "hi, hello, bye, ciao." I felt the embarrassment of traveling without speaking the language, of expecting that even in a village of 3,000, there would be someone who spoke my language. We found someone at the senior center. She was in her twenties, and wore a nearly sheer dress with a gold chain belt. She looked like a mythological Greek goddess. When we told her what we were looking for, she tried to give us directions in broken English, then gave up, opened the back door of our rental car, got in, and told us she would take us there. We'd driven past the building, but the sign outside made me think it was a hospital, and we hadn't gone in.

Inside, we met Zoltán, a man about my age, a little taller and his hair a little more gray. I explained what I came for—the marriage certificate. But even in English, I didn't say what I wanted: stories, connection, family. Our interpreter tried her best, but she could only convey fragments of sentences, of meaning. Her basic English classes had not covered the vocabulary of genealogy, the grammar of untold stories. Finally, I opened my travel notebook to the family tree I had compiled. Not much, really: just my grandparents' parents and siblings. Zoltán smiled and nodded as he said, in English, "family tree." He took the notebook and put it on his desk, put his glasses on, and leaned over to study the information on the single page. I saw him nod again. Then he pulled a pencil from the pocket of his light green short-sleeved shirt, and next to the name of my grandmother's mother, scribbled something in the margin as he spoke. Our interpreter repeated what he'd said: "She was born in Slovakia." She smiled with the satisfaction of a schoolgirl who knows she's given the right answer.

Meddig leszel itt? "How long will you be here?"

"Two days."

Jöjjön vissza két nap múlva. "Come back in two days."

Én némi kutatást fogok végezni. "I will do some research."

He photocopied the family tree.

•

My guidebook said that in addition to the thermal baths, castles are a must-see, so while we waited for Zoltán to research my family, we visited castles. From Hernadnémeti we drove to Boldogkö Castle, just thirty minutes from the border of Slovakia, suddenly interesting to me as the birthplace of my great-grandmother. I learned later that at the time of her birth, there was no Slovakia; it was all part of the Austro-Hungarian Empire.

Hungary's history, detailed by Cartledge, is a series of successful invasions and unsuccessful revolutions—a country too important to ignore, but too small to be powerful. A country that was appealing enough to be divided as a spoil of war, but struggled to be independent, its borders shifting with every turn of power, people falling asleep one night in Hungary and waking up the next morning in the same bed but a different country. First the Mongols came, then the Turks, then the Hapsburgs, and later the Nazis and the Soviets. The castles built on volcanic knolls and other rises were not the stuff of queens and fairy tales, but fortresses for protection, with watchtowers and torture chambers. We climbed the ramparts, peered through the narrow openings used to spot the approach of marauding armies while they were still far enough away to give the villagers time to gather behind the protective stone walls.

Back at our bed and breakfast, I read the history like a high school student, flipping back and forth, gathering bits that allowed me only glimpses of the story. I wondered what it does to people whose history is infused with fear and surrender. What it does to families. What it shatters.

•

I never asked my grandmother what it was like for her to leave her village and family at the age of twenty-five and get on an ocean liner with three children: József, six; Lajos, four; and János, two. Were they seasick? Was she afraid? What was it like to stand in line at Ellis Island surrounded by the babel of others seeking acceptance? What did she bring with her? What did she leave behind? I never asked her what it was like to be an immigrant in Cleveland; what it was like to lose a nine-year-old. What was it like to hold her nine-year-old granddaughter and feel the girl tense in her arms? I wonder if I'd asked, if my grandmother would have had the words to tell me.

The three boys who immigrated with my grandmother grew up, left home, and changed their last names. Two of them died young. I barely knew my cousins, who were much older.

I assumed my uncles just Americanized their names, as many immigrants did. But my father, who valued assimilation, kept his father's name. I wonder now if my uncles were motivated by something other than assimilation. I wonder now what their origin story was and what they were told it was. A stork in a chimney. Impregnation by a mythical falcon.

I imagined possibilities because that's what you do when you don't know a story. I imagined my grandfather returning to Hungary every two years to father children, and then I discarded that story because I believe if he could afford to travel, he would have sent for his wife. And all the babies were born in March, which would have meant that my grandfather, a gardener who tended gated estates in a suburb of Cleveland, took time off in June, when the grass was growing fast, the roses in bloom.

I imagined possibilities that you don't talk about with your children. I wondered if my grandmother worked as a maid while she waited for her husband to send for her, maybe for a wealthy family where the wife went to Lake Balaton every June, leaving my grandmother alone with the man of the house. Was it love? Was it what she did to keep her job?

I shift the fragments in my mind. They settle into an image of her father. But the information spins loose. There is nothing to hold the fragments and they fall apart, swirl without finding a home.

•

I was eager to see Zoltán again, to see what he might have found, even though I told myself two days wasn't a lot of time, not to have any expectations. I prepared by asking questions of an internet translation program and writing the answers in my notebook so that I could point to them and hope Zoltán would write answers that I could translate into English.

He motioned for me to sit in front of his computer. He leaned over me, looking at the screen and controlling the mouse while he loaded a genealogy program. There were thousands of names. Thousands. All with connections to this village. This was not two days of research; I'd found the one man in Hernadnémeti whose interest was in documenting the links from one generation to the next. He clicked and a photo came into view. He clicked back and then on another name, another photo, showing me something, then someone, one image dissolving into another, all too quick for me to follow. My thoughts were spinning.

I heard the bells in a church tower ring the hour. Zoltán made a selection, clicked "print," then left his office and returned with pages still warm from the printer. There was my grandmother's name. Her sisters and brother, who died as an infant. Her parents. Her sisters' children and their children's children. My relatives. Six generations—from my great-grandparents to the newest members of the clan, the same ages as my own grandchildren.

I didn't have words for what I wanted to say, so I pointed to the Hungarian words I had copied from the internet translation: *Honnan tudtad, hogy hol született a dédnagymanám?* "How did you know where my great-grandmother was born?" Zoltán smiled. He pointed to himself, then to my great-grandmother's brother on the family tree. "My," he said.

I gasped. Not surprise, but the wordless breath that escapes when the muscles around the heart let go. It was the sound of a longing being released after having been held tight for a long time. It sounded like the first breath a new baby takes.

I gave him what I had to offer in return—data—the names and birthdays of my three sisters and me, the names and birthdays of my two children, both adopted from Korea, whose untold stories of identity and immigration would not be found on these pages.

He gave me an email address for his son, who, he said, spoke English. Then my husband took a picture, and Zoltán kissed me on both cheeks, by then wet with tears.

Viszont látásra. "Goodbye."

•

On the train back to Budapest, I studied the material Zoltán gave me, shuffling the names and dates dispersed across the pages until they made stories. Aside from my grandmother, no one in my family left Hungary. Most, even in the fifth and sixth generations, listed Hernadnémeti as their place of birth, place of death, the place where their children were born. I may have passed some of them as they rode bicycles along the road or sat in wheelchairs in the senior center. One of them might have been our interpreter, who told us she longed to visit America. One of them might be paying cemetery fees every year to keep grave markers on our relatives.

I thought about how my grandmother's five children were listed, but not her grandchildren. Before my visit, my sisters and I were as unknown to my relatives who remained in Hungary as they were to us.

•

The history book says that much of the Hungarian diaspora was due to oppression or reprisals after failed rebellions. Some who left were wealthy. Some educated. Some were skilled workers. Some were Jews. My grandparents' departure placed them in the Great Economic Immigration in the decades leading up to World War I. Hundreds of thousands of Hungarians were displaced by industrialization, overpopulation, and unemployment. If things were so bad that my grandfather left for America, how did my grandmother survive during the nearly seven years that she remained in Hernadnémeti? The likely explanation is that she continued to live with her parents.

The family tree Zoltán gave me listed my great-grandmother's death as October 19, 1906. She would have been forty-eight. A few months later, my grandmother boarded the *Slavonia*, bound for America. Had my great-grandmother been ill? Did my grandmother take care of her? Was her mother the reason she stayed? Was her father the reason she left? Did my grandmother awaken in the middle of the night and see her father's silhouette in the doorway and have reason to be afraid?

What was taking shape was an image of a woman with unknown struggles and untold stories. I wonder if anyone knew her. I wonder what she would think about me asking these questions, wanting to know her truth. Would she, like the fictional Emerence, prefer misunderstanding to exposure? I wonder what it costs to live a life without choices, without language, without the intimacy that comes when people know another's suffering. How it breaks you. How you survive. I thought about how I wanted to pull away when she held me, and I wonder if I reminded her of her only daughter. I remembered how my grandmother murmured my name—"Losi, Losi, Losi"—and how I judged her for mispronouncing it. Now, in my memory, I hear the softness.

•

I continued to turn over the pages of the genealogy, piecing together patterns, counting the months between a wedding and the firstborn like a village biddy. Two years after my grandmother left for America, her older sister Magdolna married for the first time. She was thirty years of age, and I imagined her labeled an "old maid," living at home with her widowed father. The following March, seven months after the wedding, Magdolna bore a son. The man she married was the widow of her younger sister, who had died only five months before, after giving birth to their second child. I made up one story: The grieving widower has an affair with his wife's older sister in the months immediately following his wife's death. I made up another: The older sister is pregnant, the widower needs a mother for his two young children.

I focused again on my grandmother's father: two Catholic daughters whose pregnancies at the beginning of the twentieth century are clouded. I looked at the genealogy again. My great-grandparents married in January 1879, three months after Magdolna was born.

I wondered what the relatives in Hernadnémeti knew—if anyone paid to keep my great-grandfather's headstone erect.

•

Three months after I left Hungary, I saw images in the news of Keleti pályaudvar packed with Syrian refugees. Families dispersing across Europe. They traveled through Turkey, Greece, Macedonia, and Serbia to Budapest, some on foot, some in trucks, some by rail, some trying to reconnect to those who left earlier. Most wanted to get on a train to Vienna and from there to Germany. All of them looked tired—carrying all their possessions, queuing up to buy a ticket, struggling to be understood. I thought about how I found my travel to Budapest so fatiguing, my lost luggage such an inconvenience. I read that Hungary resisted these refugees and justified closing their borders with the memory of massacres by Muslim invaders. I remembered the minaret we saw near the ruins of a castle in Eger.

Those who didn't leave Hungary know the story of invaders and oppression—Nazis who sent Jews to concentration camps and sent the Hungarians who weren't Jews to be massacred on the Eastern Front. I remembered how Zoltán's genealogy had limited information about my grandmother's American descendants. Those left behind don't know the stories of those who fled, who lined up at Ellis Island, hoping to bring their education and skills to a new country, willing to leave families and language and stories behind.

•

Besieged by neighbors for most of its history, with Magyars a minority in their own country, Hungary was late to unify around its culture and always fearful of being overwhelmed by the prevalence and power of Germans and Slavs and Muslims, Cartledge explained. They made their difficult language the symbol of nationality, the core of their identity. The teaching of Hungarian—Magyar—was not required in all primary schools until 1879. And by 1898, all towns and villages had to "Magyarise" their names. Tombstones could be inscribed only in Magyar. By the time my grandmother left for America, teachers used only Magyar for instruction. The language gave them pride and a sense of connection that had been missing. Language linked my grandmother to the family she left behind but kept us from connecting.

•

I look sometimes at the photo my husband took of Zoltán and me, cousins born two years apart, a world apart, linguistically separated. There are facial similarities. But it is his body. His average height. His barrel chest. The way he wears the belt of his trousers, a narrow belt worn a little too high. So like my father.

In the photo I am smiling, and it is not the smile of tourist snapshots, but a smile of mouth and cheeks and eyes.

•

But for the shame of immigration, the shame of sex—maybe incest, maybe rape—the shame of my grandmother speaking English poorly, the shame that kept my father from teaching me to speak Hungarian—Magyar—I might have stories that hold their shape. I might have known my grandmother more deeply when she was alive and have more of her to hold onto now that she is gone. I have only fragments. Not even puzzle pieces that could fit together if I turned them until I found the connections. Just scraps, like the bits of colored paper that tumble about in the mirrored end of a kaleidoscope when it's turned. But they are unstable. The bits shift again as soon as the tube is moved, the angled mirrors suggesting a new image. The fragments are not connected. There is no grammar to hold them in place.

On Finding Myself in the Old Neighborhood

I come from this lake—not just water, but the water of this lake, which has whipped Sunday sailors into submission, held the weight of barges heading to Canada loaded with carbon steel, and once belched dead perch onto the sand. I swam in this lake. I cramped in this lake. I walked out of this lake, fled from it, promising never to return, yet here I am, walking along a boulevard on its shore, watching maple trees drop golden leaves onto empty picnic tables in a park where there used to be a carousel. Here I am, with my clipboard and list of names, canvassing voters who live in red brick garden-level apartments and high rises and split-level houses, knocking until the skin on my knuckles is rubbed pink.

"Who are you?" someone yells from behind a locked door.

I am you. I am these streets, this neighborhood, this America.

I am brick. Molded from clay, transformed by fire. The strength of my form hides my porosity; I soak up water—see the salt stains on my face? I can house you, wrap my arms around you to keep you safe. Walk on me! I won't crumble. Burn me! I will still stand. Hurl me through a windshield or a plate glass window in your rage—that's how I fly.

I am maple leaf in Autumn, late to my beauty. My veins are visible now, and it won't be long before I advance to fragile brittleness and am crushed into powder beneath your feet. But for now, look at my colors—jade green deepening to black, persimmon, yellow becoming orange becoming scarlet like the yarn in an old lady's afghan. Beet red, brick red, blood red. Orange-red, like flames. See me glow as the sun gets low in the afternoon sky. Look how the rain forms beads on my skin. Stare at me, at my burgundy-tipped lobes against this brick wall that someone painted white in an effort to make it look clean and modern.

I am whitetail deer running down a wide avenue lined with brick houses dotted with cut-outs of a grinning, red-faced chief. I am wild, out of place on this street where people are awed by me and reach to touch my brown sugar hide but want me off their neatly clipped lawns where they have piled cinnamon colored leaves. You don't scare me, you waving your fan-shaped rake. There are still woods nearby where I can disappear into the maples and oaks and buckeyes, even when the leaves have all fallen and the trees are bare.

I am clouds, towering cumulus and anvil—blue-black like the barrel of a gun—clouds rolling in across the lake, wind blowing the silver underside of maple leaves into view, pressure changing, deer bedding down to be safe. I am thunderstorm. The noise of me will shake you, and you will look for the crack of my fire in the sky, wait for the rain to fall against your house. You will feel protected from me, but I will seep into your walls, leaving whiskers of white efflorescence on the crumbling brick.

I am water, rainwater and holy water from marble fonts in the vestibule of a church with windows stained with saints. I am bathwater and dishwater and sudsy water from cars washed in driveways on Saturday before the Buckeyes play. I am water in corroded lead pipes of drinking fountains in elementary schools and in aluminum bottles in cages beside treadmills. I am water flooding the storm sewers clogged with fallen leaves, flowing into a creek in a deep cut where deer drink and maples and oaks have been growing on steep embankments for generations.

"How are you?" asks the woman with a clipboard, skin the color of buckeyes and a safety vest bright as a maple leaf, when I return my rental car the day after the election. When I do not answer, she looks at the salt stains on my face, opens her arms wide as a house, and pulls me to her.

I am going home, but I want to find my way back to the lake, where it began, before I became streets stained brick red with blood; withered leaves, bundled for disposal; brown deer, running for its life; before I became the creek that divides this neighborhood from another. Before I became this America.

Boulders

We keep the wall between us as we go.
To each the boulders that have fallen to each.

Robert Frost, "Mending Wall"

D oors. Wooden doors, mostly. Some of them painted, paint-chipped, some with splintered gashes where a fist or foot landed. He puts them behind the camper, not blocking the door he uses, against the fence that divides his parents' yard from the neighbor's. Before the doors there were tables: end tables, coffee tables, colorful children's art tables. He kept these under the canopy of the camper, some on end, some atop others. After the doors there were jars. Boxes of jars. Mason jars, mayonnaise jars, jars for pickles. Stacks of boxes of jars.

The orange extension cord snakes out of the camper, keeping the door from closing completely, letting out heat and a persistent smell of beer. The cord winds around the side of the brick house where he and his brother grew up, curves around the back to an outlet on the patio. His brother owns the house. His parents rent from his brother. The camper rests on blocks in the corner of the front yard, up against the wire fence—to hold the neighbor's dog—and the adjacent laurel hedge. Just beyond the laurels, the stone steps that lead from the street to the neighbor's house. Not the people who lived there forty years ago when he and his brother climbed the mountain ash that was all that divided the properties.

•

He'd been expecting the neighbor at the door for some time. He didn't blame her. Hadn't he been the one to call the city each year when the weeds in the empty lot on the other side of the property tangled thick with blackberries? "The neighbor behind you didn't want that laurel hedge," he told the neighbor when she moved in. Later, she related how the neighbor behind let her grow tomato plants in the stretch of soil between their two driveways, the only place where the hedge didn't throw shade, and then, in late August, when the vines drooped deep with ripe fruit, the neighbor made her pull out the bushes so the driveway could be repaved. This, after sharing the home-grown tomatoes. He shook his head.

He took a deep breath when she asked if they could talk about the camper.

"Of course. I know how it looks from your front walk. I walked by there yesterday."

"I'm sure it's a more difficult situation for you than it is for me. I don't need to know the story."

But he told the story, because you always tell the story: Wife's boy. Troubled teen. Years of drinking. Enabling father. Rehab. Rehab. Rehab. "Someone always takes him in." He lived with his brother until he kicked him out. "We don't even own this property so we can't make him leave."

Another story, how he had to give the house to his stepson to settle a debt.

"I'm not asking you to make him leave. He's your family. But, maybe, a fence, a solid one to block the sight."

146

•

"Who was that?" his wife calls from the bedroom.

"Just the neighbor, telling us they'll be out of town for a week."

"Did you say her dog barks when she's at work?"

"Dogs bark. They can't help it."

•

The brother looked at the '96 Jeep Cherokee parked on the street. Plates expired. He walked around the back of the car packed to the roof with beer bottles and soda cans. Five cent deposits. He saw his stepfather looking out the window of the brick house, so he went to the door of the camper and knocked. The door opened a crack. On the other side of the laurels, the neighbor paused as she walked up the steps, one arm looped in the cloth grocery bag that hung from her shoulder. She strained to hear the conversation, but her dog heard her steps on the stones and started barking.

Species, Genus, Family, Order

Not long after the snow on our north Idaho farm began to melt for the season, the botanical ground hog that was *Iris reticulata* poked its green head out of the earth, telling me there were only six more weeks of winter. By then, the catalogs with rich images of tomatoes, coneflower, roses, lilacs, and red osier dogwood rested at the bottom of a willow basket, covered by newspapers, our orders placed and paid for, awaiting shipment. This annual assurance of new growth sustained my husband and me as we sat side-by-side, chairs pulled close to the woodstove, sometimes in easy silence, sometimes defending a choice or sharing a vision, surrendering to January's early darkness. The Greeks believed winter represented the grief of Demeter, Goddess of Grain and Growth, after her daughter Persephone was abducted by Hades and taken to the Underworld. Demeter's depression caused the fields to wither, fruit to dry up, the ground to appear barren. Only when she struck a deal for her daughter's annual return was there the flourishing of fertility, the rebirth we call spring.

My garden selections centered on perennials. I was drawn to the certainty, the continuity from one summer to the next that roses, coneflowers, and chrysanthemum would return, even if the price that I paid was that I could only enjoy the blossoms briefly. I shied away from sowing seeds each spring. Either none of them germinated or more came up than my garden could accommodate, and I could not bear to sacrifice any. My choices arrived already started, fragile seedlings held in moist peat pots.

My garden was where my grown daughter looked for me when she wanted to talk. She would perch on a basalt boulder at the edge of the grass, hugging her knees, her brown skin deepening in the sun, her wavy dark hair a genetic mystery. I might hand her a bucket of weeds to dump or ask her to turn on the hose, but my desire to work the soil came from a heritage that I couldn't impose on her.

•

Center stage in my garden were hybrid tea roses, the variety introduced in 1867, which is the demarcation between old roses and modern roses. Roses date back to the estate of Josephine Bonaparte, to the monasteries of Benedictine monks, to the Persian gardens 5,000 years ago. Old roses, prized for their vigor and fragrance, exhibit seven unique scents: nasturtium, violet, apple, lemon, clove, tea, and something that only can be described as rose. Shakespeare said, "That which we call a rose by any other name would smell as sweet," but a unique name had to be found for that singular scent, and it is rose. In the eighteenth and nineteenth centuries, gardeners hybridized roses, breeding them in an attempt to create perpetual blooms with layers of petals and high centers and colors other than pinks and creams. The fragrance often was surrendered. The most beautiful rose in my garden may have been Opening Night, forest green foliage against deep red petals that hold their color for days, extravagant blooms on long stems. But it makes a liar of Shakespeare.

A rose can be cloned easily by rooting a cutting or grafting it onto any strong rootstock. Propagating a rose from seed is more difficult. Seeds from the hips of a hybridized rose will yield surprise varieties, nothing that looks like their mother.

My roses began blooming tentatively in June, then picked up steam until taking a break at the peak of summer heat, returning in August until stopped by heavy frost in September or October. During the rush, I filled my sink with ice water before heading to the garden with shears, cut the stem of the chosen blossom at an angle, and submerged the entire cutting in the ice water before cutting the stem again under water. After this shock, the rose would do what I wanted: open slowly, filling the house with scents of citrus and musk. I admired their ability to survive extreme weather and rough handling without losing any of their delicacy.

•

From my garden I could see my husband squatting in the pasture examining a clump of orchardgrass before heading off to the job that paid for the farm. Grass looks like grass to me, but he knew the stiff fingers of orchardgrass, the drooping spikelets of brome. He grew species that were drought-tolerant and thrived in cool weather, and he could tell the moisture content of a blade by caressing it between his thumb and index finger. He chose each species for its unique characteristics. Orchardgrass was palatable when it first emerged—especially to livestock that have been feeding all winter on hay. Bromegrass was appetizing later in the summer. Wheatgrass is livestock's Brussels sprouts, only worth eating when everything else is gone. My husband planted it on the most eroded acres of our hilly land in an effort to limit grazing.

For my husband, the land and the grass and the animals on the grass were one organism. The soil held the nutrients that sustained the plants that nourished the animals. When he held a clump of orchardgrass in his hand, he saw the calf that later in the spring would be hidden there by its mother.

I planted flowers for quick reward; he planted grass and trees for longevity.

One year a horticulturist told my husband that our climate was ideal for black cherry trees. If the trees were pruned to direct growth to the trunk rather than the branches, in twenty years we could harvest the wood. My husband envisioned an orchard of richly grained bookshelves, Merlot-colored cabinets, polished coffee tables. He ordered three hundred seedlings.

The trees and roses we ordered in January arrived each year near our son's April birthday, when the temperature was still cool enough for successful relocation. Too much heat initially can produce a plant that appears to thrive but has insufficient roots to store nutrients and support its growth.

The cherry trees arrived a few days after a surgeon had opened my husband's knee to remove a piece of loose cartilage torn in a fall. With my husband unable to kneel, it fell to me to plant the seedlings while he supervised, feeling impotent. The day was cold and breezy, and the clay soil was compacted with spring rain and the remnants of winter snow. It clung to the spade like chilled cookie dough. Every now and then I had to pause and scrape it off the shovel with my bare hands. My fingertips blanched with the cold and wet.

After I planted each tree, I tamped the ground around it, collapsing air pockets where moisture could collect and freeze around the tender roots. I could see my husband ached to handle the saplings, but he could only lean on his crutches planted on the sloped hillside and watch, reminding me over and over: "Don't expose the roots to the wind."

•

Before I had a rose garden, I grew vegetables, like my father and grandfather before me. My grandfather had been a professional gardener. His own garden began just a few steps from the back door of the house he had built himself: rows of pumpkins and acorn squash, beans and tomatoes tied to rough-cut poles. As a child, I ate those tomatoes like apples, plucking them from the vine and biting into the dense flesh, the orange-red juice running down my arm and dripping off my elbow. When our family moved to a new city, my father dug a vegetable garden in the back of our house, planted tomatoes, and when we moved again, he repeated the ritual.

My first vegetable garden was in the back yard of a fourplex my husband and I rented when we were in school. A photo in an album shows my husband leaning against the garage, embracing a shovel. We'd begged permission from the landlord to dig an eighteen-inch-wide piece of earth and nursed six tomato plants from seedlings, staking them as they grew. We knew when we planted them that we'd move before the fruit ripened, but it didn't matter. This is how we claimed space, made it our own.

Some fifteen years later, not long after we'd moved onto our land, I turned the dirt on the south-facing side of our house into a vegetable garden with raised beds I built myself. I filled them with carefully measured proportions of topsoil, sand, compost, blood meal, and bone meal, concocting a balanced environment of calcium, phosphorous, nitrogen, and potassium. I turned the mixture over and over, placing the spade into the dirt and stepping on the ledge of it, until the loam and the bone and stench were one.

When the soil was ready, I planted: basil and oregano and sage in peat pots that I started inside under ultraviolet light; sugar snap peas and red leaf lettuce early from seed; zucchini and spaghetti squash a little later; red peppers, Japanese eggplant, and finally, Roma tomato seedlings when I was certain there was no chance of frost.

For a few years, we had fresh salads, well-seasoned chicken and fish, and an August of zesty stews made with peppers, tomatoes, and eggplant. But the growing season in our microclimate was too unpredictable, too short. There were too many rows of green tomatoes hanging in the garage each fall.

The rich soil and the cool climate, I decided, were better suited to roses like those my mother planted wherever we lived.

Despite my own passion to reproduce the gardens of my youth, I discouraged my husband from propagating our farm with the hardwoods that reminded him of his origins—oak, maple, and hickory—trees that grow slowly, live forever, and drop richly colored leaves in the fall. I'm fond of them, too, but I didn't want to be like the early settlers of the West who brought cuttings of their favorite eastern plants with them, trying to make the strange open spaces of the West look familiar. I didn't want a farmhouse that pretended it was in Ohio. When my husband showed me a small hickory tree, I placed my hands on my hips before passing judgment. "Put it behind the barn where I can't see it," I told him, as though it was a rusted old bicycle. He ignored me.

One day I looked out the kitchen window, across the lawn and partway into the pasture, and saw him watering the tree. We squabbled over its location for a few days until he finally looked me in the eye, and with his chin set, said, "I want to be buried on this farm, beneath a tree like the ones we had in our yard when I was growing up." He looked away before continuing. "And I want it to be in a place where you'll see me when you look out the window."

My husband was in good health, but as we moved into the second half of our lives, I understood not only his thinking about his own mortality, but the desire to have a sense of continuity-- to bring his past to his present and imagine it his future. When we got married, my husband left the house he had lived in since he was one year old. He'd helped plant the hickory and maple in the front yard and measured his own growth with theirs. My family moved frequently. I learned to adapt to new environments. I did not become attached to a particular house, but to the gardens my parents created wherever we settled. When my husband planted hardwood trees and I planted tomatoes and roses, we were reproducing not just vegetation, but our histories. We were thinking of heritage and legacy, of unbroken chains, in broader ways than people do when they have biological children, because we had to.

•

When I first began replacing vegetables with roses, I wasn't particularly selective. I bought whatever appealed to me in those glossy winter catalogs. Individually, the flowers were attractive, but the garden wasn't. In truth, it wasn't just my garden that was unsatisfactory, but my life. My daughter had left home for college; my teenage son was pushing me away. My husband had retreated to the far edges of the farm, mending every fence but the ones that needed it most. I felt burdened and boxed in. One day I took a crowbar to the raised beds. Grunting, I wedged the lever under the wood and released each box from the soil that had compacted around it in contrast to my unwillingness to release myself from my responsibilities. I lugged the boxes to the pasture, then collapsed in the dirt. Lying there, I felt the warmth of the soil on my back, smelled the humus I had stirred up and was reassured of the life-giving nutrients still in the earth.

I redesigned the garden, enlisting my husband and son to do the heavy work. I watched the two of them digging and hauling, communicating the way men do, over tools and muscle and sweat. Then I smoothed the rigid edges where the boxes had been, mounded and shaped the soil into irregular islands. All that summer, I carried flagstone, fitting them together like a jigsaw puzzle in sand placed over a layer of fine, compacted gravel, creating clay-colored rivers flowing around islands. When I had left all the weight of that summer in the garden, I swept the stones.

I filled those islands with carefully chosen varieties of roses--blush pinks, silvery blues, robust purples, nearly black reds, and deep corals. I bought Rio Samba for the joy of yellow petals that turned to orange along an edge as ruffled as the skirt on a salsa dancer. I bought Peace for its name and Billy

Graham despite its name. I bought some for their dignity, some for their fortitude, and some for their attitude. I bought Sunset Celebration for the way its pinks bled into its oranges, Mr. Lincoln because it smelled the rosiest of all roses, and John F. Kennedy for sentiment. I planted then tenderly, piling peat moss and soil into a mound and arranging the roots over the mound as though untangling a young girl's hair. The new garden did not follow the template from the past, but a vision of the future, like the one that had brought us to the farm in the rolling Palouse hills of the Idaho panhandle.

This unique landform was shaped six million years ago by deposits of windborne soil—called loess—from the Columbia River Basin. The hills look like dunes covered in wheat or peas or barley. But after those crops were harvested, the stubble turned under, and the ground tilled for next season's planting, there was nothing to keep the fertile soil from being carried by the spring's snowmelt into creeks and rivers. Around the time we moved to our farm, farmers started receiving a sufficient financial incentive to change those farming practices, but before that, the Palouse had some of the most eroded hillsides in the nation. We bought fifty-six acres of them.

At first glance, the land had little to recommend it. With the exception of some scrubby bushes in a draw, the place was treeless. We looked at those scoured hillsides and saw pine trees cradling quail. Where rich topsoil had washed into a depression on the southeast corner, we saw a pond with small-mouthed bass, heard the echoes of bullfrogs on a summer night. When we allowed ourselves, we saw a young boy swinging on a tire roped to a tree limb, a little girl floating on the water in an inner tube.

We set about reclaiming the soil, planting grass to hold and revitalize it while providing a home for pheasant, quail, and Hungarian partridge. We dug the pond and hauled the loam that had been deposited there up to the barren knoll where I imagined the garden. My husband planted 150 fast-growing yellow pine. We spent years readying the land before building a house, finally moving to the farm when our children were seven and ten years old.

.

We began looking for a child about the same time we began searching for land. We had known even before we married that I might not be able to conceive. We tried anyway, and the foreknowledge of infertility didn't lessen the pain. "We'll adopt," we said glibly, before experiencing the human drive to reproduce. After we had grieved for the children we would never have, the ones we assumed would embody only the positive traits we loved in each other, the ones who would keep our DNA in the gene pool, we created a new vision of family.

Our children are from Korea. My people are from Eastern Europe; my husband's are from Poland and Italy. All our ancestors, though, are in the earth.

As a child, I slapped mud into patties, coiled bits of colored clay into pots and plates. I ran barefoot, feeling the warmth of the ground or its cool smoothness as it squished between my toes. As young lovers, my husband and I picnicked beneath a buckeye tree, stretching out on the grassy slope. I have stood in reverence as a loved one was returned to the ground, reaching to place a single bloom on the coffin that held their remains, a rose connected to the those of Babylon and Mesopotamia, the cradle of civilization.

Still Life with Birds

In January the birds get tipsy. You know that moment in the long stretch of winter when the holidays are over and there's nothing to distract you from the darkness and bleakness and the never-ending grind of feeding yourself and keeping warm, and the snow that continues to fall and drift.

The cedar waxwings mass on a telephone wire near the mountain ash, now bare of leaves, waiting for the boots on the kids walking to the bus stop to stop crunching, not unlike the stay-at-home mother who waits, peeking from behind the kitchen curtains before turning to what will distract her or give her day a bump or soften the feeling that she is slipping away, getting smaller, the way the bus does as it gets to the end of the road, before it completely disappears.

When the yellow bus is gone, and then one day, the children themselves, it is still. You are alone with the day. With the chores that must be done and the guilt when they're not done and the story you said you'd write or the friend you said you'd call or the still life you said you'd paint or the life you said you'd live. You sit at your loom and look at the scarlet warp yarn wrapped there for months, or at your piano, where you note the waxen skin on hands that rest on yellowed keys. Your eyes drift to the window.

The snow topping the cedar rails of the fence is piled high, undisturbed. It looks firm, permanent, dignified even, but all it would take is a child running a red wool mitten along the top to tumble it to the ground where it would be just more snow. You see the waxwings, acting as one, descend on the mountain ash and gorge on berries that are slightly frozen, a little sugared, a bit fermented. Avian ice wine. You want to tell the birds to pace themselves, but you would only scare them back to the wire, and why begrudge them this folly now, so deep into winter?

After the easy berries are gone, the bird bodies twist and contort, reaching toward more distant branches for glossy, smooth fruit the color of fire. The birds try not to lose their grip, but after all those berries, one slips. You watch it land in the snow under the ash, stunned, watch it shake the snowflakes off its pale brown head and the yellow tips of tail feathers. You wait to see if it will fly back to a branch or settle where it is.

The birds strip the tree, like an old woman picking her savings clean.

Wings

By then she knew that when she was scared she invented stories: The red maple in the front yard would fall when the wind came from the north. The red-tailed hawk roosting in the fir tree would snatch the cat. The acetone-soaked rags would ignite, and the easel and the canvasses and the brushes would flame red then settle into gray on a moonless night.

The fear would become fire and she would write it on her skin.

All that spring, her skin had burned with worry. She put ice on it. She rubbed cocoa butter into it. She cooled it with liquor. Lots of Scotch. She peeled off the scorched flesh at night and stuffed it under her feather pillow. Then she lit a candle and wrote again on the raw, pink pulp left behind, a story to explain and soothe.

One morning she awakened in the coral light of pre-dawn, certain the maple tree had fallen so hard its roots were exposed, shredded by the upheaval. She sniffed the air for smoke, listened for the click of flames engulfing her studio. Her skin prickled. Panicked, she called the cat.

Enough.

She laced up her hiking boots.

She hit the trail hung over, weaving up switchbacks on a sandstone monolith the color of salmon swollen with the ache of ripe eggs. She left heavy footprints in the soft stone powdered under thousands of boots like hers, pilgrims who had come to the desert for rebirth, thirsting and fasting and longing. Beside the path, she saw the vestiges of spring's wildflowers, cliffrose and paintbrush, withered in the occasional patches of shade.

Her mouth was dry. Her teeth held grit. As she climbed, she licked the inside of her cheeks.

She climbed for an hour, or maybe a day, or maybe longer, before coming to a broad, false summit before the trail narrowed over a slice of rock that connected the massive body of stone she had just ascended with another that rose nearly vertically from the canyon floor. Hikers stopped on the flat, sat in small groups to eat their sandwiches. They swallowed water and made excuses for not going on. She stood, looking at the scene as an Impressionist might have, the Sunday afternoonness of friends and families picnicking together, oblivious to danger and love.

Her breath was shallow from the elevation gain and groundless fretting. She wanted a cigarette. She hadn't smoked in years. But she thought if she sucked on a cigarette, the muscles in her lungs might remember how to expand and fill, and she could exhale the anxiety that settled in the space below her sternum like dirt in the corners of a room.

She sat away from the others, took off her hat and swept her face with her white bandana, which then looked bloodied from the rust-colored dust and sweat streaked in the crevices etched by dread.

She ate a grape.

Took a sip from her water bottle.

Something fluttered. A bird. Her stomach.

Below, the river wandered through the desert canyon, shaded even at midday. She watched from above as a falcon rode a thermal, then stooped in what looked like a free fall. The bird brought its prey up to a narrow outcropping on the wall that rose from the river to the point she could reach only by the slender trail—the point, the map said, where angels land.

She marveled at the vision of raptors. She couldn't fathom seeing with such precision, to be able to discern a mouse or a ground squirrel from 1500 feet. She wondered what would be different if she could see that clearly.

After resting on the flat, she stood, hoisted her pack onto her back and turned to the rocky spine that led to the apex. She waited until the hikers descending from the top were off the single track. At the end of the queue was a woman, her gray hair poking out of a khaki fishing hat. The grosgrain ribbon that served as a hatband held a brown and white striped feather—not a feather that came with the hat, but one she must have found. The skin on her face was worn and sunburned, like that of a snake ready to molt. The old woman stopped beside her, reached up to her hat and plucked the feather, then handed it to her, as though returning something to its rightful owner, before continuing down the path.

She tucked the gift between her breasts and stepped onto the bony path. Below, on her left, the river twisting through the valley. On her right, hikers making their way from their cars to the switchbacks.

She picked her way gingerly, one boot in front of the other, one sandstone vertebra at a time. When she reached the end, the sweat on her skin felt cool.

After the spine, a climb up steps ground by the soles of strangers. She boosted herself over boulders and through crevices. At the top, a few trees sculpted by wind.

She walked to the edge. Across the canyon, red rock layered with white and gray. Over time, sediment had been transformed by time and pressure into stone: ancient sea beds to limestone, clay into shale, desert sand to sandstone.

The afternoon sun lit the uppermost stratum. She sensed an updraft. She inhaled deeply and stretched her arms to their full wingspan. She knew if she leapt, she would fly.

The Scent of Water

Vaux's. Rhymes with hawks, but these are swifts, the smallest of swallow-like birds.

End of summer, the swifts trek south: Oregon, Central America, Venezuela. Picture them: backs of gray and brown feathers, sickle-shaped wings. Cigar-shaped bodies the length of my middle finger. Weight: one-half ounce, the heft of a pair of maple samura, winged seeds that fly like helicopters.

The family name for "swift" is derived from the Greek word *apous*, without legs, because the swifts fly continuously, not stopping to eat, even copulating in the air. They rest only when nesting, incubating eggs long and white, and at night, roosting in the hollows of old growth snags and in chimneys like the one at Chapman Elementary School in Portland, Oregon, the city that is now my home.

One evening in mid-September, my husband and I joined hundreds of others spreading blankets and setting up low camp chairs on the grassy hillsides of the Chapman school grounds, waiting for the spectacle of some 30,000 birds swooping into the flue. In between sips of white wine and tastes of chicken salad, we scanned the sky for the first sign of the birds. What at first appeared to be an unorganized flock became increasingly ordered with each pass they made of the chimney. We cheered like soccer fans when one of the swifts broke away to chase off an opportunistic hawk circling overhead. Then, just at dusk, they dropped into the opening one by one, and we joined the rest of the spectators in a single exhale: "Ohhhh."

The birds have returned to that smokestack each September for almost forty years, like an old man might pull into the same family-run, low-slung motel year after year, with its faux wood paneling smelling of cigarettes and Pine Sol, the car parked right at the door marked with a single digit. There are more modern hotels, more modern chimneys. Chapman's furnace has been replaced; the original brick one there only for the birds now, stabilized with wires. Even an earthquake won't shake them loose from this ritual, this return, the call to come home.

•

"Homing," says naturalist Bernd Heinrich, is the search for "our own good place," a nest suitable for raising our young and the surrounding territory that supports that endeavor. And the orienting and ability to return if we are displaced.

When our daughter was eighteen months old and our son still a longing, my husband and I bought fifty-six acres of bare hilly farmland because when we stood on the slope where we planned to build a house, we imagined hundreds of yellow pine defining the border, a pond where geese would stop on their migratory journeys and where the croak of bullfrogs would echo off the hills. We saw an orchard with apples, peaches, plums.

The farm was a dream formed when my husband was in medical school and one of his professors invited his students to a picnic on his land just outside the city. The redbud were in bloom. The frogs croaked. The professor drove a tractor that pulled us in a hay wagon to the creek, pulled us into the dream.

We built that house, dug that pond, planted those trees:

Five thousand yellow pine *(Pinus ponderosa)*.

Three hundred black cherry *(Prunus serotina)*.

A one-and-a-half-acre pond, uncounted resident bullfrogs *(Lithobates catesbeianus)*.

An apple orchard *(Malus pumila)*.

We divided the land into pastures with metal fences and bought four domestic elk—one bull and three cows—elk because my husband loves elk and because they are efficient animals, impacting water and land resources far less than cattle. We didn't know our pastures disrupted the path the wild elk took in the winter to search for food when the high country was deep in snow. Sometimes the wild bulls tore at the fence with their antlers, determined to stay on their historical route, the one their ancestors took long before farms and fences, the one that is written on their bones. But a fence designed to keep something in is also effective in keeping that something out. The wild elk gave up and walked along the outside of the fence until they could again locate the markers, find the scent that put them back on their way to their winter home, where generations had found food and safety.

Christmas 1996. I woke first to the filtered light that said snow had fallen overnight. I went downstairs and piled kindling in the woodstove, crunched newspaper, laid logs of tamarack, lit a match. Standing in front of the stove, letting it warm me, I looked out the front windows. Snow continued to fall like stardust. Three elk pawed the snow down to the grass. My breath caught for a moment at these reindeer relatives appearing on our front lawn on Christmas morning, then my chest tightened. The yellow tags in their ears meant these were not wild elk, but ours, my husband's fear of their escape realized.

We rounded up the elk easily. There were no historical routes for them to find—all of them were born in our pasture, and while animals have homing mechanisms, they can't use them if they don't know where they are when they start out. That year's calves, six months old, had not followed the rest of the herd through the gate that had been left open; their scent beckoned the adults, reminded them that home is where it is safe to raise your young.

·

From second-floor windows in our house, we could see beyond the front yard and down the hill to a pond the size of a football field, surrounded by cattails. In the spring, Canada geese nested in boxes my husband built, planted at the edge of the pond and filled with hay. We watched for signs the eggs had hatched, saw fluffy goslings pushed by their mother between the slats of the goose box land in the water. They followed their parents in a downy parade into the high grass, a safe harbor from predators until the chicks could fly. We believed they would return one day with their mates to raise their own goslings.

In the fall, when the tamarack across the road yellowed, dozens of geese landed each night at dusk, rested on the water overnight—sometimes close to a hundred. I heard them again just before dawn, the signal for me to go to the window. I imagined them negotiating with one another about the direction they would take off on for the next leg of their migration. And just as the sun rose above the eastern horizon, they would lift off as one, still chattering, their wings banging against the air with the effort to raise their heavy bodies. Picture one: back of brown feathers, black neck, white chinstrap, wingspan as wide as I am tall, each bird the weight of 250 Vaux's swifts.

A few hardy geese hung around all winter. I never wondered why, but perhaps they had malfunctioning migratory mechanisms, had been displaced and no longer knew the way home. One night, when a long period of sub-freezing temperatures without snow or wind created ice smooth and deep, we walked down the hill to the pond, skates slung over our shoulders—mother, father, daughter, son. I'd learned to skate on just such a pond, in a golf course near our house, my father holding my mittened hand. That night the moon was full, the sky cloudless, but fog collected in the curve of the land where the pond was. We circled in the filtered light, able to see only a few feet but knowing the edges, as though skating in a dream. I crossed my outside leg over my inside to make a turn and there, in front of me, was a family of geese, setting on the ice, heads tucked under wings. I skated around them, trying not to disturb their rest. The pond was their home.

During my son's adolescence, when he ignored parental warnings about dangers, rejected guidance, safety, us, I held onto the memory of that night, the lightness I felt gliding on narrow blades across water that had become solid when crystals bonded to create a seamless surface. The ease of it. The trust. So when, at dusk on a spring day just before he turned sixteen, my son called to me from his second-floor bedroom in what sounded like his eight-year-old voice: "Mom, the geese are back," I felt a certainty settle in my chest: he would return too.

•

Deuterium. Heavy hydrogen. An isotope that marks a dragonfly's place of birth.

Most of the hydrogen atoms that bond with oxygen to make up water have only a proton on their nucleus, but a small fraction also have a neutron. This is what makes it heavy. It's called deuterium because it has about twice the mass of hydrogen, although the origin of the word, *deuterios,* means "second place."

Every ocean, lake, river, pond contains a known amount of deuterium, based on its latitude. The amount of deuterium in rain falling in the Bahamas differs predictably from that in snow falling in Bismarck, North Dakota. Some think all the deuterium came from comets.

When a dragonfly nymph hatches, it soaks up the deuterium

of its first home, taking the stuff of shooting stars into the segments of its abdomen, the wing buds on its thorax. The water the insect is born into becomes part of its tissue forever, carried in the body like the one that flits across the surface of the water where I kayak, my boat the shape of a dragonfly, my paddle moving like wings. By analyzing the deuterium in an adult dragonfly, wings like the tail of a comet, scientists can know roughly where it was born, but the dragonfly knows it in its body, finds its way back to where it was born, knows corporeally when it is home.

The common green darner *(Anax junius)*.

Black saddlebags *(Tramea lacerata)*.

Wandering glider *(Pantala flavescens)*.

Spot-winged glider *(Pantala hymenaea)*.

Variegated meadowhawk *(Sympetrum corruptum)*.

Not all dragonflies migrate—in fact, only a fraction are known to, but these five are among the North American species that head south in the fall. They leave what has been their home, but is not their birthplace, when cold weather makes their habitat unable to sustain life, to provide protection or food. They often travel in swarms, becoming easy marks for hungry migratory birds along the way, the survivors returning to their natal waters where they lay their eggs and die.

•

I was conceived, my mother told me unsolicited, during a family vacation on Presque Isle, a narrow spit of sand jutting into Lake Erie. She had recently miscarried. *Presque* means "almost." I was almost not conceived. *Deuterios.* Second place.

I wonder what I carry in my tissue that tells me I am home.

The feel of the wind lifting maple leaves to show their silver underside before a thunderstorm.

The scratch of a sharp blade on smooth ice.

The filtered light when I open my eyes that tells me new snow is comforting the ground.

The scent of water—of perch and diesel and Coppertone—as I push off the sandy bottom of Lake Erie, level my body, begin to kick like a dragonfly nymph.

•

When I was seven, my family moved from the Ohio shore of Lake Erie to Colorado. My parents told me there would be mountains. I drew a picture of individual peaks, inverted Vs side by side. I colored them blue with a uniform cap of white at the top of each. I didn't understand the complexity of geological formations, of foothills and canyons and ridges, but the wonder of landscapes created by glacial floods and tectonic shifts has never left me.

For the next few years, I could see the highest peaks of the Rockies from our yard, from the road, from the playground at school: Mount Evans. Mount Warren, Rogers Peak. They lay to the west, my North Star, a reference point for finding my way home.

Ants and bees, monarch butterflies and some birds navigate by using the sun as a compass, adjusting their flight patterns as the sun's position changes throughout the day. The indigo bunting is among the birds that use the night sky for orienting, fixing on constellations as they rotate around the North Star. Whales and dragonflies rely on landforms for homing. But these navigation systems are far more complex than a simple visual recognition of familiar signs and patterns. Heinrich says the sophistication of homing mechanisms and the sheer physical performance of birds and insects traveling such distances was for centuries considered impossible because it was so superior to anything humans themselves could do. Humans, who rarely ventured far from their birthplaces, did not develop an evolutionary need to home.

I question how true that is. What accounts for the feeling of *coming home* reported by so many descendants of African slave trafficking when, generations later, they return to their motherland? What prompted hundreds of pioneer families to head West, finding their way with descriptions of landforms, to what they believed would be their *own good place*? How do we know where to go when a place no longer sustains us? How was it that the Rocky Mountains instantly felt familiar to my seven-year-old self?

•

When my family went to the mountains—on Sunday afternoons or when relatives visited from Ohio—I collected rocks from the creek beds where we stopped to eat the sandwiches that Mom packed. Most of the rocks I pocketed were quartz—smoky, pink, clear—or unremarkable granite, or granite with bits of quartz or mica. Once I found a slab of solid mica an inch thick and six inches wide, with smooth translucent layers like the surface of a frozen pond. I peeled off the sheets one at a time, like onion skins, unaware that their hexagonal atom structure made that possible, unaware that the word mica was influenced, in part, from the Latin *micare*, to glitter. I took those bits of the mountains home with me, nestled them in the cotton of my mother's discarded jewelry boxes, learned their names. Took them with me when we moved back to Ohio.

I married a man from Ohio. A man who took me to swim with him in Lake Erie and to skate on a frozen pond by the yellow light of a Coleman lantern. Early in our marriage, I urged him to visit Colorado where he saw mountains for the first time. We decided to move to the West, to Idaho where we would buy a farm and start a family. Our *own good place*.

•

One summer, after our son and daughter were grown, dragonflies swarmed me, their iridescent blue bodies glittering like mica in sunlight. They followed me, landing on my bare shoulders shimmering with sweat as I walked the bike path near our farm, far from any body of water large enough to account for such numbers, the heat rising from the asphalt, the smell of ripe wheat being cut.

That August, I woke with breath that was frozen. The farm, where we'd lived for sixteen years and where our children had swum in the pond and lain in the grass to watch shooting stars, felt uninhabitable. My husband and I were on divergent paths, unable to find our way back to one another.

Without a homing instinct, says Heinrich, humans find their way when lost "by maintaining a constantly updated calculation for at least two reference points, and the motivation to use them." My husband and I had not updated our calculations, or maybe we lacked the motivation to use them.

•

In mythology, dragonflies represent change—the kind of change that results from maturity and the deep diving that results in breaking through illusion to self-realization.

•

That August, my daughter and I drove south to where my son and his fiancée lived. "We thought we'd all get tattoos tomorrow," my son said, like I might have planned a trip to the mountains with out-of-town guests, packed sandwiches to eat beside the creek.

I went first. I gave the tattoo artist an image of a dragonfly from an aboriginal painting. It reminded me of a visit I'd made to Australia ten years before. I'd ignored advice and gone into the bush, the backcountry, to hike a trail beneath an undercut. Far from my home, I sought out a wild place where I learned how to be by myself.

I sucked in my breath as the needle pierced the skin on the inside of my ankle, watched the blue-black ink stain my skin, the dragonfly becoming part of me.

"What will dad say?" my daughter asked.

I don't care.

I said it, and the thought lifted me up.

A few months later, I left the farm, unsure where my next home would be, but feeling in my bones that it was time for me to move on. Find a second place.

•

More than a year later, my husband and I hiked a trail in the Columbia Gorge. We took a side trail to the shore of the creek, peered into the water to see salmon the color of sandstone cliffs, bellies full of ripe eggs. I might have known only this one fact about animals when I was growing up—that salmon swim upstream, miles and miles, from ocean to mountain streams like this one near Portland, to find the place where they were born. They are moved to lay their eggs in a spot that has already been proven to generations before them to have the gravel necessary for nests, called redds, water with sufficient oxygen, food where their young can feed safe from predators. But I didn't know that salmon smell their way home, following the scent of water, the fragrances that first met their olfactory glands when they were born. Only a small percentage lose their way over a journey that may cover hundreds of miles, their memory of smell misguiding them to a sister stream. Almost.

My husband knew, the way an elk that has gone astray knows how to find its herd, I was not coming back to the farm, even after the two of us found a way to be at home again together. He pointed us west, as I had done early in our married life, and we landed in Portland, Oregon. The Willamette River that divides the city into east and west smells of algae and moss. Mount Hood lies to the east, its volcanic energy like a tuning fork that tells me we've hit the right note. My new North Star. To the west is the Pacific Ocean, where the salmon spend the bulk of their lives before returning to their natal waters.

•

Eight years later, I sat eating my lunch, looking out on the waters of Lake Erie. The grass, still green despite the lateness of October, was filled with sparrows on their fall migratory path. Each morning, in the blue hours before dawn, volunteers walked the downtown streets, looking for birds whose internal navigation systems had not alerted them to a tall office building. They were scooped up, and when possible, taken to a rehabilitation center for care. I wonder, when they were released, if they found their way home again.

I was in Cleveland to help get out the vote in the weeks before the 2016 election. I told the recruiter who named the swing states needing volunteers that I was born in Cleveland, and that seemed as good a reason as any for me to be assigned there. It was my first time back since my parents and my husband's close relatives had all passed away. My first visit by choice, not duty. When someone behind a locked door asked me who I was, what I wanted, I would not just say that I was a campaign volunteer, but that I was from the neighborhood, born a few streets over. It was my way of saying *I belong here.* And I knew it was true because of the way my feet kicked the maple leaves, scarlet and blood-red and orange, as I walked from one house to another. I knew it was true by the way the lake smelled of perch while I sat on its shore, eating my lunch.

Works Consulted

Belenky, Mary Field, Blythe McVicker Clinchy, Nancy Rule Goldberger, and Jill Mattuck Tarule. *Women's Ways of Knowing: The Development of Self, Voice, and Mind.* New York: Basic Books, 1986, 1997.

Berkenwald, Leah. "Ten Things You Should Know about Rose Pesotta," *Jewish Women's Archives,* March 1, 2011. <https://jwa.org/blog/10-things-you-should-know-about-rose-pesotta>

Cartledge, Bryan. *The Will to Survive: A History of Hungary.* London: Hurst & Company, 2011.

Goldin, Claudia, and Kenneth Sokoloff. "Women, Children, and Industrialization in the Early Republic: Evidence from the Manufacturing Censuses." *The Journal of Economic History,* 42, no. 4 (1982): 741–74.

Heinrich, Bernd. *The Homing Instinct: Meaning and Mystery in Animal Migration.* Boston: Houghton Mifflin Harcourt, 2014.

Kanter, Rosabeth Moss. *Men and Women of the Corporation.* New York: Basic Books, 1977.

Lonely Planet, Steve Fallon, and Anna Kaminksi. *Budapest and Hungary.* Lonely Planet, 2015.

Myss, Caroline. *Sacred Contracts: Awakening Your Divine Potential.* New York: Three Rivers Press, 2003.

Pfeiffer, Bryan. "The Nuclear Option for Dragonflies," September 11, 2014. <https://bryanpfeiffer. com/2014/09/11/the-nuclear-option-for-dragonflies>

Robinson, Harriet Jane Hanson. *Loom and Spindle: Or, Life among the Early Mill Girls.* T. Y. Crowell, 1898. Available for free on <books.google.com>

Szabó, Magda. *The Door.* Translated by Len Rix. London: Vintage, 1987.

About the Author

 **Lois Ruskai Melina** is a writer and retired educator. She was the editor and publisher of *Adopted Child* newsletter and the author of three books focused on helping parents understand the impact of infertility and adoption on families formed by adoption: *Raising Adopted Children, Making Sense of Adoption,* and *The Open Adoption Experience* (with Sharon Kaplan Roszia).

For her book *By a Fraction of a Second,* she followed nine elite women swimmers for eighteen months leading up to the 2000 US Olympic Trials.

After receiving a PhD in Leadership Studies from Gonzaga University in 2008, she taught leadership at two universities. Her research focused on social movements and the performance of leadership. She was the lead editor of the anthology, *The Embodiment of Leadership.*

She lives in Portland, Oregon, with her husband where she enjoys rowing on the Willamette River and following women's soccer. She has a grown son and daughter and two grandchildren.

SHANTI ARTS

NATURE ▪ ART ▪ SPIRIT

Please visit us online
to browse our entire book
catalog, including poetry
collections and fiction, books
on travel, nature, healing, art,
photography, and more.

Also take a look at our highly
regarded art and literary journal,
Still Point Arts Quarterly, which
may be downloaded for free.

www.shantiarts.com

CPSIA information can be obtained
at www.ICGtesting.com
Printed in the USA
JSHW022112010221
11327JS00007B/101